TENNIS PLAYERS AS WORKS OF ART

TENNIS PLAYERS AS WORKS OF ART

DAVID LINEBARGER

atmosphere press

CONTENTS

INTRO: US OPEN

Louis Briel, *Arthur Ashe*, 1993. Acrylic on canvas.
National Portrait Gallery, Smithsonian Institution;
gift of the Commonwealth of Virginia and Virginia Heroes, Inc.

ARTHUR ASHE,
ART BY LOUIS BRIEL

Solve this problem: Your daughter's playing with a doll, a gift she just received from a friend. The doll is white.

1968: John Carlos's black power salute Arthur Ashe wins the first US Open. 1970: Toni Morrison *The Bluest Eye* the problem of "whiteness" as a standard of beauty Arthur Ashe wins The Australian Open. 1972: Bettye Saar *The Liberation of Aunt Jemima*. 1975: Ashe beats Connors to win Wimbledon *no matter what I do, or where or when I do it, I feel the eyes of others watching me, judging me.* Arthur avoids tennis clubs where he is not allowed, skips tournaments he cannot enter, turning and turning, as contemplative, as inward as Rembrandt, his favorite artist. In Rembrandt's *Aristotle Contemplating a Bust of Homer*, Ashe sees the *close kinship between admiration and envy* he must feel when contemplating John Carlos or Muhammad Ali—black athletes who could protest in ways Ashe's personality and patriotism would not allow. Ashe, always soft-spoken and behind the scenes. *The problem with you, Arthur, is that you are not arrogant enough* (Jesse Jackson). White racists told Ashe how to live. Black activists told Ashe how to live. Should he take the white doll away from his daughter during a nationally televised benefit for the Arthur Ashe Foundation for the Defeat of AIDS the year before his death? Does the burden of race weigh more than the burden of AIDS? In his excursions to South Africa to play tennis, Ashe did as much as anyone to challenge the system of apartheid. Nelson Mandela in prison reads *A Hard Road to Glory*, Ashe's three-volume history of the black athlete. Ashe cannot abide any sacrifice of dignity, any sacrifice of morality; the question always always always *How can a black person live a life of freedom and dignity?* Mandela in America, smiling that smile when someone whispers Ashe's name in his ear. *Ah, Arthur is here.*[*]

---

[*] Much of the material here is taken from Ashe's *Days of Grace*

"Ever since that day when I was 11 years old, and I wasn't allowed in a photo because I wasn't wearing a tennis skirt, I knew that I wanted to change the sport. I wanted to use sports for social change."

– Billie Jean King

Christina Tarkoff, *Billie Jean King*.

BILLIE JEAN KING[*],

ART BY CHRISTINA TARKOFF

PARABLE OF THE THREE DOORS

The first door is locked. Dead bolts everywhere, a not-yet-discernible voice inside. *I couldn't get a closet deep enough. I've got a homophobic family, a tour that will die if I come out, the world is homophobic and, yeah, I was homophobic.* The second door is a ceiling. The Houston Astrodome, the stars. Some call it Title IX. King still wakes up nervous, then realizes she won. *I thought it would set us back fifty years if I did not win that match.* An athletic and creative strategist who knew the value of taking risks—her aggressive serve and volley style had won her eleven Grand Slams—King decided the day of the match to slowball Riggs, run him as much as possible. DON'T DO THAT! THAT'S CRAZY! Riggs jumps over the net, shakes her hand. *I really underestimated you.* The third door is opening, open. The third door is closing, closed. You try to open it. Someone else tries to open it. Before the door stands a doorkeeper. She shakes your hand. *Hi, I'm Billie Jean King.* Who speaks next? What do they say? How can we open more doors?

---

[*] The US Open's main facilities are named The Billie Jean King Tennis Center and Arthur Ashe Stadium in honor of these two champions who expanded rights for all peoples.

I: SIX WOMEN

Lady Pink, *Serena Williams*.

LADY PINK PAINTS SERENA WILLIAMS

"It's not just a boy's club. We've got a sisterhood going."
– Lady Pink

Badass. That's what I say to my daughters. That's what they say to me. We repeat it for emphasis in hushed tones, reverence: *Serena's a badass.* Diva of high notes, fashion. Built like a brick house in tight black leather. Her powerful body in a leopard skin dress as it prepares to pounce on a weak second serve. *Badass.* She serves almost as hard as half the men—and with accuracy, placement, disguise. How many women pitch in the big leagues? That's what Serena's serve is. Who cannot love her much-maligned father? Every day his children had to fill an empty page with reflections, thoughts. Here are some of Serena's notes to read to herself during matches: *Attack the short ball—it's waiting for U!!! U R black and U can endure anything. Endure. Persevere. Stand Tall... U R part of the strongest people alive. Nothing is worse than what your grandparents and great-grandparents went through. Nothing is more difficult. Nothing. Get up, get out, and make yourself/your people happy and proud!* Who could possibly bring such thoughts to life on a tennis court? Thank you, Richard Williams. Thank you, Oracene Price.

Lady Pink, the "First Lady of Graffiti," paints Serena against a pulsating background of bright-cool-lipstick-loud colors. These are not delicate scrolls of rococo seashells in living rooms of decorative grace, but half-spirals/whorls/lines of female creative

energy, self-expression, political rebellion (always remember-
ing self-expression for a woman—especially a woman of color—
was/is a politically rebellious act). The crown placed deftly atop
Serena's head is a female descendent of the crowns Basquiat
bestowed upon his male boxers and musicians who were role
models of self-expression and self-determination in the black
community. Now Serena wields her racquet like Muhammed Ali
his mouth and fists, Charlie Parker his lightning sax. *Be yourself.
Move forward.* That's what I hear Pink's portrait shout, though
not quite as loudly as one of Queen Serena's primal screams on
court. *The old rules of exclusion were made to be broken.* Joy Harjo
(Muscogee/Creek), our current Poet Laureate, provides the cau-
tionary/celebratory tale: *Crucial to finding the way is this: there is no
beginning or end. / You must make your own map.*

Mark Winter (Chicane), *Martina Navratilova,* **Autographed Sketch.**

MARTINA NAVRATILOVA, THE HEROINE WITH A THOUSAND FACES,

ART BY MARK WINTER (CHICANE)

Thesis. In what many observers consider the greatest rivalry in the history of sport, Chris Evert and Martina Navratilova helped change societally constructed ideas about female identity. Chris Evert proved that you could be an intensely driven professional woman and feminine at the same time. Martina, well, Martina's the missing heroine in Joseph Campbell's *The Hero With a Thousand Faces*. Her story (herstory) mirrors the archetypal hero's journey in all the world's myths and religions.

I: Departure, the Call to Adventure. One of the first prominent athletes to risk defecting in secret from an Eastern Bloc country, Martina left her family behind reading the newspapers: *Martina Navratilova preferred a fat bank account.* Her call to adventure included American freedom, its endless opportunities, its many doors of ice cream, fries, Big Macs, Whoppers... Won the first three of her eighteen Grand Slam singles titles as *The Great Wide Hope* (Bud Collins).

Mark Winter's Comments: I have been keen to get a signed Martina sketch for a number of years. She is a permanent fixture during The Championships at SW19 these days, as a commentator and competitor in the Invitational Doubles, but has remained elusive, until yesterday (July 1, 2018), when I happened to be hanging around Gate 13, as one does on the day before 'hit-off' and she happened to walk out and down the road with a purposeful stride, followed by a handful of devotees in hot (30 degree heat) pursuit. Mission accomplished.

II: Initiation, the Road of Trials. *I never thought there was any-thing wrong with being gay.* To say one was a lesbian was to turn one's back on the holy trinity of money, fame, virtue. Martina's life as a private-becoming-public lesbian. Martina's life as an Eastern-Bloc-defecting- private-becoming-publice-motional-yet-intellectual-yet-devil-may-care lesbian. Add to that the most challenging question: *How do I beat Chris Evert?* So workouts, weights, diet. A complete body makeover like the kind you only see on TV. Once Martina married her hard-earned athleticism to her imaginative skill for attacking the net on lefty serves, big forehands, and biting knifed back-hands, what could poor Chrissie do? What could anyone?

III: The Hero's Return, the Public "Boon." Not true in the case of our heroine! Martina never returned to us; we finally caught up to her. We now hold these truths as self-evident: that you can love who you want to love, that you are what you eat, that female athletes lift weights, that getting older does not mean you must stop competing. Martina won the Wimbledon doubles title a few months shy of her fiftieth birthday. Just as many early feminists saw Eve not as a sinner but as a hero-ine who challenged the status quo, someone who by reaching for the fruit of greater knowledge broke the patriarchy's rules and was punished for disobedience, Martina's now a heroine for many. Martina's mainstream now.

Brooke Hunter, *Suzanne Lenglen and Antoine Watteau.*

SUZANNE LENGLEN AND ANTOINE WATTEAU'S *PILGRIMAGE TO CYTHERA,*

ART BY BROOKE HUNTER

Imagine Lenglen playing tennis in a hidden corner of Antoine Watteau's *Pilgrimage to Cythera*. Dressed more lightly than the crowds of spectators in their rococo frills, her body is both concealed and revealed in all its ballet. A breast can be glimpsed or imagined. Lenglen's every tennis stroke a musician's glissando or dancer's glissade guided and placed as if on a handkerchief on her opponent's side of the court. (Her father trained her using real handkerchiefs.) Performance pressure? When she feels too much, she sips a little cognac on changeovers. Watteau's lovers in attendance are thrilled, dazzled. Their lovemaking later will be enhanced and forgotten, the island's reigning sculpture of Venus displaced by a real-life Goddess of the homely. As the other great players of the 1920s described her: *You can't imagine a homelier face* (Helen Wills). *Heaven knows no one could call her beautiful* (Bill Tilden). But Lenglen as Goddess, nevertheless. Goddess as mystique, as popular song. The classic WWI song, "There's a Long, Long Trail," became a Lenglen trail of spectators winding more than a mile to see her at Wimbledon. Did Louis the Sun King have that? Goddess meaning she smoked and drank through six consecutive Wimbledon singles titles. Goddess meaning tennis as ballet to the music of Lully, Rameau. The absolutism of Louis XIV gives way to the rococo dreamscapes of Watteau. WW1 gives way, a memory. Suzanne Lenglen conquers France.

Miki de Goodaboom, *Steffi Graf.*

I like how the bright pink background of Miki's portrait of Steffi contrasts with the black of Rothko's late paintings and my one-sided, darker portrait of Steffi.

STEFFI GRAF AND MARK ROTHKO,
ART BY MIKI DE GOODABOOM

I picture her alone before a late Rothko painting, his darkening palette. Steffi's favorite color was black. Rothko's floating color field, *a universe for viewers they do not have in the real world.*[*] Black a type of protection; a barrier against stalkers, reporters, celebrity, noise. Black a tunnel, a cave, a hole, a portal. The inevitable turning toward light, the quest for tennis perfection. How do you enhance a gazelle-like sprinter's speed, a skidding knifed backhand that rarely missed, the power and precision of the greatest forehand in the history of women's tennis? Steffi racing fast-forward to whatever was next: the next serve, the next point, the next changeover, the next tournament. Black the color of mourning, of grief. The father she loves in prison for tax evasion related to Steffi's earnings, that crazy misguided stalker assailant stabbing Monica Seles to help Steffi become #1. Emotions *intimate and human.* Limitless space, the sublime. *Silence is so accurate.*

---

[*] All italicized portions are quotations from Mark Rothko.

Miki de Goodaboom, *Monica Seles Dream.*

MONICA SELES,
ART BY MIKI DE GOODABOOM

Randomly choose a number from 1-4.

1. Better if the violence happens offstage as in Greek drama. Just give me the plot, the facts. The nine-inch boning knife, the deranged fan of Steffi Graf coming out of the stands, the attempted killer walking free. Catharsis means the purging of pity and fear, what spectators should feel. Ok, ok. I just felt stunned, and then, like everyone, I went on with my life. Monica Seles? Wasn't she the one who was stabbed?

2. One by one, a whole bag of Oreo cookies. Run a dozen 400 meters back to back, then train for three hours more. What's on TV? What's in the fridge? Are there any Pop-Tarts left? Overeating one way to cope with violence. Raped, stabbed, depression, doubt, numbness, withdrawal... How many struggle against demons we guess at but never know? How many, like Monica, come out free and clear on the other end?

3. The joyous all-out control-abandon-release of her ground strokes. The two pitched (uw whee) of gruntscream gruntscream gruntscream. Two hands on both sides, the forehand indistinguishable from the backhand. No one hurled more arms legs body mind propeller hips shoulders pinwheel buzzsaw grunt backhand scream forehand scream ferocity joy crazed ball machine double time triple time missiles torpedoes. Monica's game like a military weapon that even Leonardo with all his imagination could not have invented for the women's game.

4. 1991-1993 captured seven Grand Slams. Three straight French, three straight Australian. Youngest ever in history to win the French Open at sixteen years old. Ranked #1 in '91 and '92. If not for being stabbed on the court in 1993, how many Grand Slams would Seles have won?

24

Chris Evert, Newsweek Cover, June 26, 1972. ©Al Satterwhite.

CHRIS EVERT,

PHOTOGRAPHY BY AL SATTERWHITE

Of the five greatest female tennis players of the modern era—Margaret Court, Chris Evert, Martina Navratilova, Steffi Graf, Serena Williams—who was the one good athlete? Easy to name the Amazons: Margaret, Martina, Steffi, Serena. That leaves Chrissie, and if we take pure athleticism out of the equation (can we do that?), she is easily the best player who ever lifted a racquet. Average mover. Average power. But no one ever struck the ball more precisely and consistently than Chris. And that perfect, teachable technique. *Training the body to obey the mind*, as Chris herself put it. Due to her classical good looks and feminine style, Evert was often unfairly depicted in stereotypically gendered terms. Early on she was *America's Sweetheart*, a *Cinderella in Sneakers*. After winning and winning, a cooler, cruel wind: *Ice Princess, Ice Maiden*. In the 1970s and 80s, how many girls wanted to be like her? How many men fell in love?

AL SATTERWHITE ON HIS PHOTOGRAPHS
OF CHRIS EVERT

Newsweek sent me to photograph Chris for an upcoming cover story. Since she lived not far away, it was easy to meet up with her and her father, who was her coach. They had a home court where I could set up a blue seamless paper backdrop for the cover. Evert was fun and very easy to work with during the

> Al Satterwhite on this Newsweek cover: "I'm not in love with this because it was for the cover & they wanted a bluc background, although they masked it out a little."

shoot, so I jumped at the chance when *Time Magazine* asked me to shoot her for their cover. The *Newsweek* cover ran later that month. The *Time* cover never ran as it got pushed due to the necessity to cover news events of the moment. It's always a joy to work with young athletes as they are always energized and eager to work with you. They sometimes come up with great ideas to make for a better picture. It's always difficult to pick a favorite photo. I like this photo because it shows the real-life Chris when she was having fun as we were bantering back and forth between setups for the cover.

Chris Evert, Black and White Photograph.
©Al Satterwhite.

This is Al Satterwhite's favorite shot of Chris Evert from the two photoshoots he did with her.

II: FIVE MEN

Hazel Soan, *Federer at Wimbledon.*

ROGER FEDERER AND MYRON'S *DISCUS THROWER,*
ART BY HAZEL SOAN

When the ancient Greeks sculpted the victors of an Olympic event, the goal was to produce not the athlete itself but the perfect, idealized image of the athlete, the body in *rhythmos*, the discus throw imagined as god-like, eternal. In Myron's *Discus Thrower*, the arms fully extended to their perfect still point form a perfect arc through the shoulders, the human body infinitely more graceful than a tightly drawn bow the moment before release (what classical meant when people knew what classical meant). Yet the key to all this potential power is in the core, the legs. How they twist and turn in perfect balance, the entire musculoskeletal system a flexible chain. As in Myron's *Discus Thrower*, so Roger Federer on every shot. Tennis not how it's played, but how we imagine the gods might play it. The serve, the forehand, the one-handed backhand drive. Grace, beauty, fluidity, perfection. Statistics can be boring: Most Grand Slam singles titles, most weeks at #1, etc., etc., etc.... How about that shot in the heat of a point that set Federer apart from all the others: the mid-court ball, which he attacks with his forehand, the footwork almost invisible, light tiny dancer quick floating sudden whip of the forehand into one of the opponent's corners to dramatically change the point. I could go on and on about Federer. Watch his second serve in slow motion. How high he gets off the ground, the perfect balance of the legs, the racquet slicing across the ball at an extreme but elegant angle. Let's just put up a sculpture in the public square. Better yet, maybe a series of ten sculptures for ten different shots: the flick backhand pass, the scissors kick overhead, the short slice backhand crosscourt... Might even include a tweener—no one hit it better. Is the sculptor alive who could do Federer justice? Could Myron?

HAZEL SOAN ON PAINTING ROGER FEDERER
(FACEBOOK POST, JULY 14, 2019, LONDON)

Watching Wimbledon today—breathtaking tennis. Last year I was lucky enough to see Roger Federer play at Wimbledon early in the tournament. This week I couldn't do anything else but paint this watercolour of him from one of my photos of the match last year. To get his likeness I finished it during the semifinal against Nadal on Friday, holding it up against the TV until I recognised the figure on the screen had materialised on my paper. Love that moment of recognition in portrait painting.

Sam Brannan, *Rafael Nadal.*

RAFAEL NADAL AND THE LASCAUX CAVE PAINTINGS,

ART BY SAM BRANNAN

35

4,500 rpm on the forehand. Borg's topspin revolution doubled, squared. All that topspin means net clearance, safety, angles. The perfect weapon for clay, its wars of attrition. Not far from the arena of Roland Garros lay the caves of Lascaux. In the womb of their history lay hundreds of familiar, mysterious beasts. Rafa's afraid of animals, the dark. He sleeps with his lights on at night. Before each match he seeks rituals: chants, mind games, order, control. A cold shower focuses the mind. He wraps six racquets, watches like a boxer as his hands are taped. He stares at the walls, remembers, rehearses. *Go without, do more. Endure. Get every ball back. Endure. Do not be afraid to take risks.* The words of his Uncle Toni. He sprints back and forth. *Vamos, vamos.* Let's go, let's go. The plural "we" is important; his entire family, his team, is involved. He ties on his bandanna, jumps up and down. Anything to deliver the mind from fear. Fear of winning, fear of losing, fear of injury. Childhood's broken bone in the foot, the patella, the tendons of this knee, that knee. Play with pain, conquer fear. Spill your guts every point. Sweat. Take your time between points. The drip, drip of sweat.

Victor Jerez, *Novak Djokovic.*

NOVAK DJOKOVIC,
ART BY VICTOR JEREZ

One. Two. Three. Four. Five. Six. Seven. Eight. Nine. Ten. Eleven. Twelve. Thirteen. Fourteen. Fifteen. Sixteen. Seventeen. Early in his career, the most irritating ball bounce in the history of tennis. Changed that. Early in his career, major trouble with heat, breathing problems. Went to a gluten-free diet. Early in his career seemed dark, brooding, misunderstood, Eastern European, never really liked much, Ivan Lendl 2.0. Then hilarious imitations of Rafa, of Sharapova, to the US Open crowd at night. Djokovic the Joker. Then perspective, world citizen, graceful speeches after losses in Grand Slam finals. Then sheer excellence. Twenty-four Grand Slams and counting. No one can hit that one shot he hits when pulled out wide on the backhand side: Gumby backhand impossible power consistency the left leg sliding on harsh concrete its sudden plant slide stability does the left hand provide all that power is it coordination Gumby flexibility Chinese acrobats Russian circus performers somehow still able to hit a forcing shot everyone else—Everyone else!—has to hit a one-handed defensive sliced backhand. Add impeccable movement that squeezes the court on his side. Add the most consistent ever well-struck deep down the middle return off 130 mph serves to begin the point. Add his entire arsenal of powerful, precise ground strokes that rarely miss like all those bombs dropped on Milosevic's Serbia when Novak as a child searched for a safe, quiet court to play on.

Scott Kish, *Bjorn Borg.*

BJORN BORG
AND THE NORSE GODS,
ART BY SCOTT KISH

39

I wanted to be Ringo Starr one year for Halloween. Long hair, girls screaming, rock star. A few years later I wanted to be Borg. Long hair, headband, topspin, rock star. No one burned as brightly for five or six years. The Angelic Assassin, beatific like the beats, then simply beat, burned-out, retired at twenty-six. Five consecutive Wimbledon titles. Four consecutive French Opens, six overall. The best on grass like Sampras or Federer, the best on clay like Nadal. Best on the fastest surface. Serve and volley, attack. Best on the slowest surface. Patience, long rallies, endurance, ground strokes. Never before a human being like that. *They should send Borg away to another planet*, said Nastase. *We play tennis. He plays something else.* Racquets strung so tight the strings break, ping like guitars or violins in the middle of the night. *Is I magen (Ice in the stomach).* Pulse rate in the thirties, a myth, of course, like the stories of Odin, Frigg, Thor, Balder...

Sam Brannan, *Pete Sampras.*

PETE SAMPRAS AND NIRVANA,
ART BY SAM BRANNAN

Remember your first funeral? Pete put his first Wimbledon trophy in his coach's casket. Earlier he broke down and cried between points and games in the 1995 Australian Open quarterfinals against Courier before somehow winning the match. Tim Gullickson, brain cancer, gone. Each grain of salt vanishes, becomes the cosmic ocean. Hinduism 101. The problem in Hinduism is that this essential truth lies hidden beneath a magical yet deceptive illusion of surfaces (*Maya*) that deceives us, distracts us from understanding. The problem for sports fans when contemplating Sampras was much the same. Pete's tremendous competitive will—*the strongest-willed athlete I've ever seen* (Paul Annacone)—lay deceptively buried beneath the veil, the veneer of a superb classic athlete, someone who made everything look easy: his all-court game, his running forehands, his gift of history's best big clutch serve. On fast courts, especially, opponents were dispatched too easily. Spectators grew bored, the headlines cruel. Samprazzzzzzz would put you to sleep. How many are awake enough to see beneath life's surfaces? How many might be enlightened? The answer in Hinduism is that everyone will be. Just give it enough time, enough lifetimes.

III: CHANGE

Ted Dimond, *Venus Williams.*

VENUS WILLIAMS,
ART BY TED DIMOND

The older Venus Williams as Duke Ellington at the piano. Keep your solos understated, perfect. Let others in the orchestra stand out: the saxophone, the trumpet, Serena. Yet for the first half of her career, it was Venus's tennis that screamed lead trumpet. All the other women over six feet tall who won Wimbledon—Davenport, Sharapova, Kvitova—moved in the freeway's slow lane while Venus gobbled up turf as if on the German Autobahn. Great speed, great height, great power. Those are the scary athletes. Ted Dimond's *Venus* captures her staggering power and presence. Motion everywhere. Energetic, dynamic brushstrokes. The racquet twitching, another impossibly huge serve about to happen. The stenciled *"US Open"* in white flies apart at the edges while Venus's extended left arm seems half like a flagpole anchoring a huge American flag in the stands. This flag represents both the crowd's excitement and this new, evolving United States that Venus and Serena helped create. But what happens as you age, as health problems emerge, such as Sjögren's syndrome? What will happen to those millions of young girls, especially girls of color, who see themselves, their possibilities, in the way you carry yourself? What is grace? What is beauty? When arguing for equal pay at Wimbledon, keep your solos understated, perfect: *The message I like to convey to women and girls across the globe is that there is no glass ceiling.*

Scott Kish, *Andre Agassi.*

ANDRE AGASSI'S WIG,
ART BY SCOTT KISH

At dawn I sighed to see my hairs fall;
At dusk I sighed to see my hairs fall...

Did Agassi lose his first French Open final because he was worried his wig would fall off? *Image is everything.* Vegas, entertainment, the flashy shot. When the going got tough, his beautiful zen-like-deer-in-the-headlight eyes. How to explain those eyes and hands, his return of serve? Childhood's father boxer creates dragon monster, a souped-up ball machine spitting fastballs, curves. Hit or be hit. Children must defend themselves. Timing can be learned. Slay the father by becoming the father. Tennis as boxing. Ground strokes as body blows. Train. Train. Meditate. Train. Run hills in the heat, bench 300 pounds. Serve wide to the forehand. Kick it out wide to the backhand. The next shot in the opposite corner. Corner to corner. Take out the legs, the head will go. Oldest male player to be #1. Punk. Monk. Boddhisattva.

Now I know why the priest who seeks repose
frees his heart by first shaving his head.
                    – Bo Zuhyi, "On His Baldness"

Jeffrey Sparr, *Gladys Heldman.*

GLADYS HELDMAN,
A ROOM OF HER OWN,
ART BY JEFFREY SPARR

Bring me my Scotch! Tone is everything when Gladys speaks to her ten-year-old daughter Julie. *Bring me my Scotch!* Imperative, demanding, royal, and riddled with anxiety's ambition, its genetics its fire its ice, its lack of mother love multiplied by Gladys's alcoholic father of wealth, accomplishment, generosity, charm. Gladys Heldman, a brilliant woman who earned a BA from Stanford and an MA in Medieval History from UC Berkeley in just four years. Gladys Heldman, a mother of two daughters who would give birth to two more remarkable children: *World Tennis Magazine* in 1953, and the Women's Tennis Tour in 1970. At the altar of *World Tennis Magazine*, Gladys Heldman *barebreastedinbed*smokingcigaftercig Gladys Heldman a smartcrazydriven*female*inthe1950s corresponding with readers around the globe Gladys Heldman writing*editing*callingschmoozingstrategizing*rewritingTheRules*. *A woman must have money and a room of her own if she is to write fiction* (Virginia Woolf). Gladys Heldman had money and a room of her own to rewrite the reality of women's sports. Double Scotch, double Scotch, double Scotch. *I'm sorry, I'm sorry.* (That's what ten-year-old Julie said when she failed to meet her mother's demands.) I meant two double vodkas with lunch, then just before dinner double Scotch, double Scotch.[*]

---

[*] I was inspired to write this piece after listening to Julie Heldman read *Driven: A Daughter's Odyssey*, a remarkable book of insights, honesty, and terrific writing. Required reading for anyone who loves tennis and would claim to know its history. Chris Evert calls it a "must-read."

I'm touched by David's powerful portrait of my mother Gladys, and how he captured her contradictions by weaving in the power of her personality, her world-changing achievements, her nutty idiosyncrasies, and her failures as a mother.

Cat Lee (Colacat), *Ons Jabeur.*

ONS JABEUR
AND THE ARAB WORLD,
ART BY CAT LEE (COLACAT)

53

Young Arab women in twenty-two countries practice Ons Jabeur drop shots of outrageous height and spin. It's about having the right feel. It's about having soft hands. Girls in Tunisia and Algeria practice tweeners and trick shots like the one in Colacat's artwork. Girls in Iran and Iraq learn to dictate points instead of waiting to see what happens. A girl in Bahrain becomes proud of her body, her two strong arms. She starts lifting weights as girls in Egypt do planks in the sand and a girl in Syria tells her grandmother about Ons Jabeur. They watch a match together. They laugh, they shout, they cry. In one girl's room in Somalia, the harm and hurt of social media turns soothing, spiritual. Ons on Instagram and Ons on Twitter: big hugs and smiles with opponents after matches. Girls in Yemen and Jordan and Morocco think others might be friends, not enemies.

Miki de Goodaboom, *Gigi Fernandez and Natasha Zvereva.*

GIGI FERNANDEZ AND NATASHA ZVEREVA, 1 + 1 = 14,
ART BY MIKI DE GOODABOOM

Wins and Losses: Fourteen Grand Slam doubles titles together in just five years. After a big loss, they danced and splashed in the water like kids. After a big win, they gleefully ripped off their tops, revealed the first sports bra to the world.

Natasha: I imagine Natasha reading *Anna Karenina*, Tolstoy's late-nineteenth-century plunge into the meaning of Russia, the meaning of life: *Happy families (or doubles teams) are all alike; every unhappy family (or doubles team) is unhappy in its own way.*[*] Natasha the first athlete to demand that Russia let her keep a portion of her earnings. The year was 1989. Was it Perestroika, Glasnost, Gorbachev? Or was it a courageous young woman named Natasha, and many like her, who helped move history along?

Gigi: She jokes she's the slacker in her Puerto Rican family of doctors, lawyers, artists... When she was nine years old, her father hit tennis balls at her from service line to service line. Gigi defended herself, gradually developing the quickest reflexes and best volleying skills in the women's game. No doubles championships without that. In the face of immense social pressure about what a young woman should do or be, Gigi became the first female professional athlete in Puerto Rico, the first and only Puerto Rican to win two Olympic gold medals.

---

[*] The famous opening line (with my additions) of Tolstoy's novel.

The Partnership: In their joint Hall of Fame induction speech, Natasha thanked Gigi for *mentally opening her up* as if something in Gigi's fiery personality helped Natasha plumb new depths of joyous creativity and spontaneity that matched both her philosophy of life and her ability to hit any shot with any spin from anywhere on the court. Add to Natasha's creativity and consistency an aggressive, competitive player like Gigi, who is always moving/poaching/faking and looking to pounce on any weak shot from the other side. Those KGB agents would have never had a chance.

NOTES

From an email from Gigi Fernandez: *We started playing [together] in 1992. Just 3 years prior, before the "wall came down," this would not have been possible since Russian tennis players were constantly followed by KGB operatives and were only allowed to play with other Russians.*

Shawn Adair, *Our Last Go Round.*

58

FOUR AMERICANS AT THE LITTLE ROCK CHALLENGER,

ART BY SHAWN ADAIR

They come to Little Rock from all over the world: Australia, Ecuador, the Bahamas, Canada, Portugal, Argentina, Colombia, Japan, India, Barbados, Chile, the Dominican Republic. They come to fight for points.

Ryan Harrison, recovering from elbow surgery, must arrive five days early and win a Wild Card tournament of thirty-two players just to get into the Little Rock Challenger. He wins it, then immediately loses in the first round, earning 520 dollars and 0 points. Ernesto Escobedo is killing Donald Young in the first round; he seems clearly the better player to the naked eye. After losing a point, Donald rockets a ball into the unsmiling sky. *I'm quitting this sport*, he shouts. Now thirty-one years old, Donald Young reached a career-high ranking of #38 nine years ago in 2012. No way he gets there again.

Escobedo plays Jack Sock in the second round. Escobedo stoic throughout as a Roman warrior while Sock mumbles to himself. Escobedo's expression never changes after he hits big booming serves and forehands for winner after winner after winner. His expression never changes after having numerous match points before losing to Sock in three tiebreaker sets. 7 points, 1,000 dollars.

Sock wins three more close matches and the tournament, his first win in four years after struggling with injuries. It's a big moment before hundreds of fans in Little Rock. He earns

7,200 dollars and 80 points. Five months later he is ranked #157 in the world. He still must play challenger after challenger after challenger.

Welcome to Little Rock. Welcome to Orlando, Las Vegas, Charlottesville, Knoxville. Welcome to Bratislava, Milan, Lima, Guayaquil...

PLAYER BIOS:

Ryan Harrison, 29 years old, current ranking #557, career high #40 (2017)

Donald Young, 31 years old, current ranking #346, career high #38 (2012)

Jack Sock, 28 years old, current ranking #248, career high #8 (2017)

Ernesto Escobedo, 24 years old, current ranking #188, career high #67 (2017)

Carol Jacobsen, *Althea Gibson.*

ALTHEA GIBSON
AND BASQUIAT'S BOXERS,
ART BY CAROL JACOBSEN

A sharecropper's shack, Daddy working the fields. He wanted a boy but got Althea. Is that why they boxed on the rooftops of Harlem throughout her teenage years? Ward off hard blows, give some of your own, learn to get up when you're hurt. Basquiat's boxers are black culture heroes. Joe Louis, Sugar Ray, Muhammad Ali. A young black man might crown himself. Althea Gibson? The Wimbledon crown? Tennis was not where it's at. Life as electric shock treatment. Basquiat's *Boxer* as both skeleton and flesh, skull and brain, warning and prophecy. Basquiat's *Boxer* as the sound and feel of the white world's bell that tolls its cost. How does anyone answer that bell? One answer is Charlie Parker's skittering sax solos played so fast that no one could catch them. Another answer is Ali's protest and bravado, his *swinging, not singing*, as Malcolm X said, that would win him the heavyweight crown. Dr. Eaton and Dr. Johnson taught Althea the ropes. Half the time with Dr. Eaton getting a high-class education, half the time with Dr. Johnson traveling and playing tennis. The first black player to win a major championship, Althea won Wimbledon in 1957 and 1958. Tennis, of course, could not remain a genteel white sport. As Connors put it, *tennis is boxing at 90 feet. Throwing blows at each other until there's only one man left standing.* Boxing with her father on the rooftops of Harlem, a young black woman might crown herself.

Photograph of Bob Davis, Courtesy of Bob Davis.

BOB DAVIS,
PASSING ON THE GIFT

The gift he was given was tennis. Segregation was the law in this lawless land, so the color of his skin meant many things: 1) he was not able to play tournaments and compete against his peers, and 2) he would change the world through the gift of tennis one player at a time. Thousands and thousands and thousands of players thousands and thousands and thousands of times. Introduce minority youth to tennis. Offer free medical and dental care. Offer academic support and tutoring... Obstacles? What obstacles? If you were given a gift like tennis, you pass it forward, multiply it by love and any money you could beg from those with means who were moved by your dream and the concrete reality of the many gifts you shared. Create organizations. Run them. Promote them. Be everywhere and everything at once. Meet and greet. Write and write and cheerlead and schmooze. Have your racquet ready. Your integrity, your mind, your pen. Talk the talk; walk the walk. Play the game well. Promote it better. Create opportunities where they do not exist. Find the role—the roles—for which you were born. National Program Directory for the Ashe/Bollettieri "Cities" Tennis Program, first executive director of the Black Tennis Hall of Fame. The work goes on and on. The Arthur Ashe Safe Passage Foundation, Black Dynamics, Inc., The Panda Foundation... *We developed some competitive players... maybe not world champions, but we got a lot of kids to stay in school and become productive adults. It's the most important thing I've ever done.*

IV: WAR

John Newcombe, Photograph by Robin Sellick.

TWO JANUARYS, JOHN NEWCOMBE AND GEORGE BUSH,

PHOTOGRAPHY BY ROBIN SELLICK

"George Bush once famously described Newcombe as a 'black-belt beer drinker,' his son George W. had one too many with Newk on the night he was arrested for drunk-driving."
– John Newcombe, *Newk: Life on and off the court*

1975. On New Year's Day, John Newcombe won the last of his seven Grand Slam singles titles when he beat Jimmy Connors at the Australian Open. What I loved most about the 1975 final is how Newcombe protected his weaker backhand side beneath a barrage of strategy and consistent hard serving. (Newcombe often won matches this way: mental focus, strategic acumen, huge forehands, big serves, aggressive volleying.) Observing that Connors had looked shaky smashing high lobs, Newcombe repeatedly hit high chip lobs off the backhand to keep Connors off the net. Newcombe also employed his slice backhand to hit balls low and short to Connor's forehand, making Connors hit up and generate his own pace from an awkward position. Later that year, Arthur Ashe built on Newcombe's strategy to upset Connors at Wimbledon. Later that year, the Vietnam War ended, its 58,000 American names waiting to be etched into Maya Lin's black granite mirror of the Vietnam Veterans Memorial. I graduated from high school, forgot to register for the draft.

2020. At Crystal Bridges Museum, I study President Bush's strikingly good paintings of veterans who fought in the Iraq war he ordered. I write him a note in the book of comments: *Thank you for your humanity, your decency.* President Bush, like Newcombe, a guy you might have a beer with. That's why Bush beat a wooden Al Gore, why we invaded Iraq, why I held hands in a circle with sixty others in front of the Cherokee County Courthouse the night before we invaded another people's land. That's why Wilma Mankiller, the former Chief of the Cherokee, whispered to us all, *It's happening again.* That's also why John Newcombe lived a fuller, richer life than Jimmy Connors. (I may be wrong about some of these things.) Connors too often alone in his room while Newcombe embraced, embodied the Aussie tradition of Hoad, Rosewall, Emerson, Laver, Roche... Train, train, drink, train. Spill your guts on the court, but be a good sport. Drink too many beers with your mates and laugh and laugh and laugh and laugh. Sweat it out on the court the next day.

Sam Brannan, *Karen Khachanov.*

KAREN KHACHANOV, RUSSIAN/ARMENIAN,

ART BY SAM BRANNAN

Death marches and concentration camps. Forced starvation and forced Islamization. Rapes and rapes and rapes and rapes and more than a million dead. Maybe that's not the best place to start.

My teenage daughter is recording Alexander Arutiunian's Trumpet Concerto for the National Trumpet Competition. Gypsy lyrical. Exciting, too, with plenty of showy trumpet techniques. We listen to the recording of it by Timofei Dokschitzer, the famous Russian trumpet player interpreting the great Russian trumpet concerto. Somehow I missed that Arutiunian was Armenian.

I always thought of Karen Khachanov as Russian, too. He was born in Moscow, won the silver medal for Russia in the Olympics after beating Djokovic in the Tokyo semifinals. The Russian flag always next to his name until he dropped it from his Instagram page during the Russian invasion of Ukraine. During his run to the Australian semifinals in 2023, Khachanov kept signing the television cameras with messages of support for the Republic of Artsakh. I learned that Artsakh was suffering through a blockade that deprived their largely Armenian population of many life necessities, including food. I also learned about the Armenian genocide in the First World War. How was it I never knew? Or how was it I had forgotten?

Daniil Medvedev. Photograph by James E Fawcette (c)jfawcette.

RUSSIAN STARS: MEDVEDEV, RUBLEV, AND SHOSTAKOVICH'S FIFTH,

PHOTOGRAPHY BY JAMES FAWCETTE

On the day Russia—or Putin—invaded Ukraine, the Russian tennis star, Daniil Medvedev, became the #1 player in the world. At his match that night in Acapulco, his wife, Daria Medvedeva, was seen subtly wearing the colors of Ukraine on the collar above her blouse. In Dubai at another tournament, Medvedev's compatriot, Andrey Rublev, the seventh-ranked tennis player in the world, wrote *"No War Please"* on a courtside camera after the match. His message was shown everywhere in the world. Everywhere except back home in Russia.

In Shostakovich's Symphony No. 5 (1937), he had to find more secretive ways of speaking out. He had to write music that would be approved by Stalin. As Shostakovich states about this constant pressure, *Awaiting execution is a theme that has tormented me all my life.*

First Movement: Phrases keep collapsing into repeated notes. Dead end. Dead end. Dead end. The opening tragic exchange between high and low strings collapses. The Black Marias are everywhere. Two million will be taken. No notes are safe. Shostakovich trots out a triumphant march for snare drum and trumpets rising and rising in dotted rhythms of goose-stepping soldiers. Irony? Bombast? Triumph? We know war is coming. Who cares how the soldiers march?

Second Movement: This scherzo seems punch-drunk angry or sardonic comical, each note like a Chaplinesque pie in the face of Stalin or the Russian people. Is this music for the circus? Comic relief? Shostakovich sleeps in the stairwell to protect his family at night.

Third Movement: No one's allowed to pray in public. No one's allowed to weep. At the Russian premiere of Shostakovich's Symphony No. 5, the audience weeps openly throughout the third movement. The strings divided up into choirs remind listeners of the music of the Russian Orthodox church. Is the third movement a forbidden prayer for the dead? The lone, plaintive voice of the oboe offers two three note phrases of sighs. Can anyone bear so much pain?

Fourth Movement: A long trill introduces a grotesque march led by the trombones and tubas. Just as Beethoven does in his fifth, Shostakovich ends his symphony triumphantly with a thumping ending and a turn to the major key. As Shostakovich put it, *I think it is clear to everyone what happens in the Fifth. The rejoicing is forced, created under threat, as in* **Boris Godunov.** *It's as if someone were beating you with a stick and saying, "Your business is rejoicing, your business is rejoicing," and you rise, shaky, and go marching off, muttering, "Our business is rejoicing, our business is rejoicing."*

Giada Pinna, *Kay Stammers.*

KAY STAMMERS, ALICE MARBLE, AND JFK,

ART BY GIADA ILENIA PINNA (ELY)

Kay Stammers designed her own dresses. Four inches above the knee. Is that why JFK dated her? She thought he was *spoilt by women. I think he could snap his fingers and they'd come running.* A Wimbledon finalist with a big lefty forehand in 1939, Kay was the second-best player in the world until the war snapped its fingers and everyone came running. Kay drove an ambulance, played exhibition matches for the Red Cross. It seemed everyone needed blood. She married a man who was in the Welsh Guards. Women who married soldiers never knew where they were.

Kay lost to Alice Marble in that Wimbledon final before the empire's grass grew quiet as graves. Alice married a pilot who was killed over Germany. Alice wrote she was a spy against the Nazis. Once she was shot in the back. Alice's shorts were six or seven inches above the knee. They kept climbing and climbing like airplanes in the sky to smash overheads no one returned. Kay could do nothing but watch: 6-2, 6-0. At the previous year's Wimbledon Ball, JFK's father whispered to Alice: *My girl, if you're going to win this thing, you'd better do it soon. There's going to be a war that will make all of us forget about tennis.* Soon a torpedo hit Kennedy's boat. He swam for miles and miles. Miles and miles before sleep.

Samuel Woolf, *John Donald Budge*, c. 1933, Drawing. Chalk, ink and opaque white watercolor on paperboard, 27.8cm x 24.1cm (10 15/16" x 9 1/2"). National Portrait Gallery, Smithsonian Institution; gift of Time magazine.

WATCHING DON BUDGE, ADOLPH HITLER AND PABLO CASALS,

ART BY SAMUEL WOOLF

July 20, 1937. If it happened today, it would start like this: *Hey, Don, look at this text.* Gottfried gives Budge his cell. *Good luck against Budge.* It's from Adolf Hitler. Gay and no lover of Nazis, Gottfried von Cramm will need more than good luck to avoid their punishments and prisons. Budge will later sign a letter to Hitler to plead Gottfried's case. They are the two best players in the world. Today's match will likely decide whether Germany or America will win the Davis Cup. Hitler listens on the radio while US stock sales come to a standstill. When the match finally ends, thousands stay put for almost an hour in wonder at what they have seen. They had watched Budge hit four perfect serves as he served for this first set at 5-4. They had watched Cramm hit four perfect winners off these four perfect serves to tie the first set at 5-5 all. Budge and Cramm kept lifting and lifting each other's games until history records it was one of the greatest matches ever played.

1937-1964. In the fifth set, Cramm takes a 4-1 lead. In the stands during the changeover, Ed Sullivan calls Bill Tilden a son of a bitch for supporting Cramm while Lennon and McCartney wait to be born. Budge wakes up sweating in the middle of the night for years and years with the score 4-1 in the final set. In 1938, Budge wins all four major tournaments, history's first Grand Slam. After watching Budge win the French Open that year, Pablo Casals invites Budge up to his place for a private concert. Casals must have played one of Bach's cello suites—

he was making the legendary first recording of them from 1936 to 1939—as certainly as Ed Sullivan introduced seventy-three million viewers to the Beatles' first performance on the *Ed Sullivan Show* in 1964. Budge holds at 4-2, decides on a new tactic. Since Cramm's fantastic kick second serve bounces up high to his backhand, one of the greatest shots in tennis history, Budge decides to step way in and take it on the rise, smacking each return deep and charging the net. Cramm gets a little nervous and starts missing first serves by inches. Budge breaks, then later breaks again to serve for the match. On his fifth match point, Budge hits a running, diving forehand for a winner. He takes a full page to describe it in his memoirs. No one saw the look on Hitler's face.

V: BAD BOYS

Pancho Gonzales, Tennis Multiflash, 1949.
© Harold Edgerton/MIT, courtesy Palm Press, Inc.

In 1949, Edgerton brought his strobes and other equipment to Longwood Cricket (and Tennis) Club to photograph the touring tennis stars. He was given a few minutes with each in an anteroom before they went out for their matches. In typical inventive reaction, he determined that he would photograph action outside of his brilliantly illuminated white clad body. In so many of Edgerton's best photographs, what seems like a perfect balance and form was a product of anticipation, timing, and much effort. Edgerton's ability to reveal the surprise of content with beautiful form allowed the viewer to discover more than simple visceral pleasure.

RICHARD "PANCHO" GONZALEZ(S),
PHOTOGRAPHY BY HAROLD EDGERTON

85

Edgerton's Photograph: Science, engineering, invention, art. *Time itself chopped up into small bits and frozen.*[*] 1/50,000ths of a second, then 1/50,000ths of a second. Like Leonardo's notebooks, Edgerton's photographs a scientific attempt to notate and explore the facts of life, the truths of motion: the Pancho Gonzales forehand, the wings of a hummingbird, a drop of milk falling, splashing. Through his invention of the strobe flash, Edgerton unlocked a new truth, which led to a new aesthetic vision. Photography was never the same. He said it was not beauty he was after but truth. *I am after the facts. Only the facts.* But as that other frozen moment of time, Keats's "Grecian Urn," puts it: *Beauty is truth / truth beauty.* The truth is the Gonzales forehand has never looked so beautiful.

RICHARD "PANCHO" GONZALEZ(S)

After Carlos Fuentes's *La Muerte de Artemio Cruz*

My father's bare feet, the borderlands. I could beat anyone at marbles. Practice, practice, practice, practice. The other kids kept calling me names: "spic," "spic," "spic," "wetback." Grandma said *just picture those white folks in their underwear.* In LA we lived in a kind of suburbs unknown to the Gringo world. Pancho, Pancho, Pancho, Pancho. Every one of us is a Pancho, so I beat the shit out of the best players in the world like Hoad

---

[*] Passages in italics are quotes from Harold Edgerton

and Rosewall year after year. I hated Tony Trabert the most. Played Trabert night after night after he won all the amateur tournaments like Wimbledon and the US Open in 1955. He thought I was beneath him, a high school dropout, a lazy Mexican. *You better get used to losing,* I said. I even beat Laver in my forties after he won the Grand Slam. As Laver put it, *Gonzalez gets meaner every time I play him.* Was I the best player to never win Wimbledon? Best player's true. Never winning Wimbledon's bullshit. If I played it every year, I would have won it eight times. Played Kramer's pro tour instead. Sued him, too. He never paid me what I was worth. I was handsome, powerful, dark, mysterious. Even the scar on my face attracted fans. *I won fifty points on my serve, and fifty points on terror.* That's what Kramer said. Took Trabert out to the woodshed every night.

Ken Meyer Jr., *Jimmy Connors.*

JIMMY CONNORS,

WORDS BY JOEL DRUCKER,
ART BY KEN MEYER JR.

Note: Like a monk copying manuscripts in the dark ages, I have faithfully copied the following sentences from a source with the strangest of titles: *Jimmy Connors Saved My Life*, by Joel Drucker. As I rearranged each sentence into separate chapters, I contemplated its meaning for a moment, a minute, a lifetime.

Chapter 1: "Kill or be killed."

Chapter 2: "Belleville was Sparta, a warrior's boot camp. Beverly Hills was Athens, a hedonist's delight."

Chapter 3: "I'm not Mr. Connors. That was my father. Mister this, sir that. All that formal crap."

Chapter 4: "Shove their country clubs and rich daddies right up their Protestant butts."

Chapter 5: "His game tilted toward the edge. His temperament was anti-Establishment."

Chapter 6: "Connor's unprecedented skill at hating his opponents was the rocket fuel of his career."

Chapter 7: "Connors had the guns. His biggest gun was his crosscourt backhand."

Chapter 8: "No one had ever thrown himself at every ball with such intensity."

**"Now the metal was about to come alive in ways
no one could imagine. It was time for Connors
and tennis to go electric."**

Chapter 9: "To get a stadium rocking like that is a kick you can't believe."

Chapter 10: "By the end of the decade, Connors played 15 of the 16 highest-rated TV matches in tennis history."

Chapter 11: "For the eighth and final time (more than any tennis player), Connors was on the cover of *Sports Illustrated*."

Chapter 12: "He was tennis' Elvis, its first rock 'n' roll folk anti-hero."

Chapter 13: "While Connors floated into myth, I walked in history."

Chapter 14: "When you think of Connors, cherish the fight. Cherish the struggle for survival."

Note on writing this piece: After trying many different approaches to writing on Jimmy Connors, I finally decided that I could not possibly describe Connors as well as Joel Drucker does in his book on Connors. So inspired by Borges's short story "Pierre Menard, Author of the *Quixote*," where he simply copies portions of the original *Don Quixote* by Miguel de Cervantes, I began copying my favorite sentences from Joel Drucker's book. Joel Drucker's response after I showed him this piece: "I'm honored that you've found my work a source of inspiration and creation."

Ken Meyer Jr., *John McEnroe.*

JOHN MCENROE,
ART BY KEN MEYER JR.

A PERFORMANCE PIECE

Directions:

1. Speak McEnroe's words in bold directly to another human being. These are words McEnroe yelled at tennis officials at various times in his career.

2. Imagine you are McEnroe playing the four consecutive points described below from his legendary 18-16 Wimbledon tiebreaker against Borg. Hold the racquet like a toothpick, a wand, a paintbrush…

Mac serving at 5-6 (third championship point for Borg) slices a second serve out wide Borg runs around his backhand hits an inside out topspin forehand dipping at Mac's feet Mac stretching way out low feathers a soft forehand volley into the open court **Go fuck yourself** Mac serving at 6-6 hits a hard slice first serve Borg hits a solid backhand inside-out and low at Mac's feet Mac guides a volley back deep but not deep enough Borg moves to it deftly rips a two-hander sharply angled crosscourt pass Mac lunges at but cannot reach ***You're a disgrace to mankind*** Borg serving at 7-6 (fourth championship point) Borg serves down the middle Mac hits a loopy backhand return just low enough so that Borg must volley up Borg volleys it back down the middle and moderately deep Mac hits a well-struck backhand passing shot back down the line Borg desperate to end the match barely gets a racquet on it and tumbles to the ground ***You completely fucked that***

whole thing up 7-7 Borg serves down the middle Mac rolls a forehand return low at Borg's feet Borg scoops a low forehand volley into the open court down the line and moves closer in to crowd the net Mac on the run throws up a topspin lob deep enough so that Borg can't end the point with a smash Borg hits a tough overhead back down the middle now he's back at the base line the point back to neutral Mac hits a solid topspin backhand to Borg's backhand Borg hits a soft crosscourt backhand angled near both the sideline and service line Mac moving hard to get there on the run rips a crosscourt forehand deep pinning Borg to the baseline Borg with his two-hander half-punches half-slices it down the line then sprints into net Mac races to cover Borg's slice on the dead run hits a brilliant running crosscourt backhand pass ***Get your fucking head out of your fucking ass*** speak this line *sotto voce* so that only the person you address can hear.

Jota Leal, *Ivan Lendl.*

IVAN LENDL AND THE COLD WAR,

ART BY JOTA LEAL

97

Lendl became our Boris Badenov, our Ivan Drago in Stallone's *Rocky IV*. His power baseline game seemed robotic, humorless, harsh, unrelenting—the Soviet Bloc in the Cold War era. He deformed the ball on the forehand side, welcoming the chance to smack it at close range at an opponent's head. *A man comes to net by his own risk, and should be prepared to defend it*, Ivan said. Not genteel, but effective. *Ivan, do you like America? Would you like to live here?* Lendl had seen the Russian tanks in Prague, had learned to keep quiet. Year after year, we half-created while Lendl half-played Ivan the Terrible. After becoming a US citizen, Lendl was finally free to protest: *I enjoy life. I like jokes. Nobody hates communists more than me—not even Rush Limbaugh!*

VI: NATIONAL (S)HEROES

Miki de Goodaboom, *Boris Becker*.

GERMANY, BORIS BECKER,
ART BY MIKI DE GOODABOOM

A thought experiment: let's push nationalism too far. The television stations in Germany would shift other sporting events to different times so the entire nation could watch Becker's matches. A Becker match meant drama, *Sturm und Drang*. The rocking motion before the serve, then boom. (Only Sampras had a better big serve under pressure.) The dramatic, diving volleys on grass. The Becker fist. The Becker shuffle. Becker himself said his performances on court were a type of love-making between him and the spectators: electric, erotic, power and lust, body and soul. The pre-twentieth-century heroes of Germany—Luther, Beethoven, Marx, Nietzsche—moved societies, thought. Becker was just a tennis player who happened to win Wimbledon in 1985 at seventeen years old, then repeated this feat the next year. Did a German century of defeat and shame help forge Becker into an even greater hero?[*] *Nie Wieder. Never again.* I saw these words everywhere when I lived in Germany for a year just after the fall of the Berlin Wall. In East Germany the rise of the Neo-Nazis. In West Germany they insisted I tour the camps. I watched Becker all the time on TV.

Miki de Goodaboom on painting Boris Becker: *In Germany I followed Boris Becker's career from the very beginning, with as much enthusiasm as all of the German people. It was of course a must to make his portrait!*

---

[*] A question, I realize, that is unfair to Becker. All celebrity is gloriously unfair. To what extent any great athlete—or any less important person, say you or me—should be linked to their country's culture and history is a thorny question. To what extent any country's reaction to a great athlete can be linked to that country's culture and history is perhaps, perhaps not, a less thorny question.

Tom Humberstone, *Noah/Mauresmo/Lenglen.*

THREE FRENCH (S)HEROES: YANNICK NOAH/AMÉLIE MAURESMO/SUZANNE LENGLEN,

ART BY TOM HUMBERSTONE

Miscegenation. I first read that word in a Faulkner novel. *Métisse* (mixed race). I first heard that word in one of Noah's hit songs.[*] *Half man* whispered in the women's locker room after Mauresmo came out as a lesbian. A mere decade later, a muscular body such as hers was accepted by everyone, desired by many. Truth was she played like a male ballet dancer: a Stefan Edberg, a Rudolf Nureyev, a Suzanne Lenglen, the last French woman to win Wimbledon in 1925 before Mauresmo won it in 2006. Only then could Mauresmo jokingly confess, *I don't want anyone to talk about my nerves anymore*, the nerves that too often wreaked havoc with her free-flowing all-court game. Maybe she could have learned from Suzanne Lenglen, the ballerina goddess from the flapper 1920s, who sipped brandy on changeovers to calm her nerves. Maybe a lesson from Yannick Noah, who admitted to toking up before matches. What's your biggest weapon, Yannick? *My hair, my dreadlocks.* Noah's tennis seemed carefree, reggae, creative, a spontaneous all-court game with acrobatic play at the net. When he became the only French citizen to win the French Open in the open era, he sparked the biggest party in France since the French Revolution. Three French (s)heroes head into a bar: Androgyne, flapper, two-spirit, three-spirit, four-spirit, five... *Emancipate yourself from mental slavery; none but ourselves can free our mind.*

---

[*] Discovered by Arthur Ashe in the Cameroon, Noah became a pop singer with many top hits after retiring from playing tennis.

Achille Chiarello, *Sara Errani.*

ITALY, SARA ERRANI'S TWO DINNERS,

ART BY ACHILLE CHIARELLO

1) The Fab Four of Italian women's tennis often dined together: Roberta Vinci, Flavia Pennetta, Francesca Schiavone, Sara Errani. I imagine wine flows as elegantly as their ground strokes. I imagine their laughter and smiles, grunts and groans, from a shared life together in the public eye. From 2011 to 2015, they created more history among them than any other four female contemporaries in Italy. In 2010, Francesca won the 2010 French Open with her buggy-whip forehand and endlessly creative game, becoming the first Italian woman to win a Grand Slam title. In 2012, Sara Errani was a French Open finalist in singles, reaching a career high of #5 that year. From 2012 to 2014, Sara Errani and Roberta Vinci became one of the five teams in history to win a career grand slam in doubles together. In 2015, Roberta Vinci and Flavia Pennetta met in the first all-Italian Grand Slam final at the US Open, which Pennetta won over her childhood friend.

2) Doping in Tortellini. Errani's mother a pharmacist who is trying to hide or downplay her cancer diagnosis. She's taking a drug called Femara. Somehow it gets into the tortellini. Sara ingests some of it, later fails a drug test for "Letrozole," an ingredient in Femara. For almost ten months, she is banned from playing tennis. The headlines are horrible. (In Plato's *Republic*, he poses the difficult ethical question: would you rather be innocent and have everyone think you're guilty, or would you rather be guilty and have everyone think you're innocent?) When Errani returns to tour in 2017, her service motion has fallen apart. Already short and with a shoulder problem, she can no longer toss a ball in the air with any consistency. Errani previously said her best attribute was "acceptance of suffering." Nothing to do but practice suffering again and again.

Victor Jerez, *Manolo Santana Wins Wimbledon.*

SPAIN, THE MANY GIFTS OF MANOLO SANTANA,
ART BY VICTOR JEREZ

What Pablo Casals did for the cello, Andres Segovia for the classical guitar, Picasso for modern art, Manolo Santana did for tennis in Spain. He inspired a generation who inspired a generation who inspired a generation so that every tennis aficionado knows what Spanish tennis now is—both a style that evolved and a long list of major champions: Santana, Gimeno, Orantes, Brugera, Moya, Costa, Ferrero, Nadal, Sanchez-Vicario, Martinez, Muguruza, Alcaraz...

Santana marked the beginning, the origin, of Spanish tennis when he became the first Spanish player to win Wimbledon in 1966. Both super stylish and devilishly deceptive, Santana was a maestro of creative, dramatic shot-making that kept fans on the edge of their seats: topspin passing shots, perfectly placed aces, backhand topspin lobs (a shot he invented), sudden drop shots (a shot voted the best in the game by his peers). Santana also a crowd pleaser (sometimes shouting *Olé* as an overhead whizzed by him), and an endlessly good sport who always acknowledged and thanked those around him.

Origin stories, of course, are necessary simplifications. Andrés Gimeno, Santana's contemporary, was probably just as good a player as Santana, but he turned pro and could not compete in any major championships. And origin stories are never quite true beginnings. We must not forget the numerous unnamed club players who kindly helped Manolita develop his game when he worked as a ball boy earning six pesetas a day. They might offer advice or praise, or offer to hit more than a few well-placed strokes to challenge Manolita in just the right way to encourage his development. What makes Santana's story an origin story at all is that he keeps passing the gift of Spanish tennis forward, offering his time and gifts to the younger generation: words of encouragement, a place to play, another tournament in Spain, a source of funding, the placement of just the right phone call.

The featured painting here of Manolo Santana holding the Wimbledon trophy is another gift, this time from Victor Jerez to Manolo Santana. As the artist writes on his Instagram account: *Feliz Cumpleaños Manolo Santana!! Aquí tienes mi pequeño regalo...espero que te guste!!* 🎁 🎨 🎾 *Gracias por el buen trato que me has dado siempre en @mutuamadridopen. Un abrazo muy fuerte amigo.*

My English translation: *Happy Birthday! Here's my little gift. Hope you like it. Thanks for everything you have done for me at the Madrid Tennis Masters (where Victor Jerez paints live portraits of the players). A hug from your very strong friend.*

Debra Di Blasi, *Amid the thick bamboo hides a butterfly with strong wings.*

CHINA'S LI NA,
ART BY DEBRA DI BLASI

A Chinese tennis coach to Li Na: *If I were teaching a pig, it would have learned by now. The Chinese say, A strict teacher makes for an excellent student.* In the rigid Chinese sports system, no one asked if she wanted to play tennis. Train and train, internalize the joyless, harsh voice within. After Li Na has some success, she complains, *If I have no freedom, I am going to quit.* Then *Danfei*, flying solo. After winning Grand Slam championships, she does not thank China. To the youth who adore her, she is Big Sister Na. A personality, a presence, not a communist tool for the greater good. She makes fun of her husband's snoring, his weight, his luck in finding a wealthy woman like her. In *China Daily*, the mouthpiece of the Chinese party, Li Na's "insolence" goes against "social customs and traditions." As the most marketable athlete in China's history, more people watched her win the French Open than watched the Super Bowl. Andre Agassi her favorite player. Long hair, freedom, earring, rebel. The Chinese middle class booms. Millions more play tennis, the most individual of sports. A rose tattoo's hidden on Li Na's chest. Who does not want to rebel?

DEBRA DI BLASI ON PAINTING LI NA
(TAKEN FROM HER EMAILS TO ME):

It's a bit socialist-art style, which I kind of like. (We have quite a bit of Vietnam and China socialist-style posters, prints and statues, so it was not a big leap.)

The paper, by the way, is unbleached mulberry, which I love. Slightly thicker and tougher than Yuanshu bamboo paper, with wood particles visible.

The "chops" (carved jade stamps with Xiling Red Seal Ink Paste) are: (smaller) "debra di blasi" carved vertically, and (larger) a phonetic translation of "debra di blasi" into Chinese characters, which was a gift from my husband purchased during one of his trips to China. I had a Hong Kong chop-maker create the small one for me when we lived there.

I slept on the request for relevant text and here's what I dreamed: "Amid the thick bamboo hides a butterfly with strong wings." I'm going with my subconscious.

Jeffrey Sparr, *Andy Roddick—BOOM.*

UNITED STATES, ANDY RODDICK'S SERVE,

ART BY JEFFREY SPARR

Once upon a time, some lucky prophet found a boy named Andy on a Nebraska farm... So the story might have gone in baseball lore. No one had a live arm, a fastball like Roddick. Fastest serve at the time in all the Grand Slams: Wimbledon (143 mph), French Open (144 mph), Australian Open (148 mph), US Open (152 mph). Roddick could control it, too. He served consistently at about 70% on first serves while serving between 130-150 mph. Impossible for someone who was 6'2". Impossible, but mythology happens. Roddick as American a product as Walt Whitman. Not a graceful European dancer but "one of the roughs," Roddick's feet plowed the ground with firm, heavy steps while Roger Federer seemed to float just above the earth. What Whitman aspired to be—*no stander above men or woman or apart from them*—Roddick somehow realized in a career largely defined by his losses to Federer on the biggest stages (0-8 in Grand Slam matches: four finals, three semis, one quarter). How did it feel? *It was miserable. It sucked. It was terrible... Except for that, it was fine.* Except for that serve, that blazing live arm, Roddick was one of us.

Leonardo Luque, *Pancho Segura's Forehand.*

ECUADOR, PANCHO SEGURA,
ART BY LEONARDO LUQUE

Rickets. Poor. Ecuador. Dirt. His two small hands sweeping, picking up balls at the Guayaquil Tennis Club while cruise liners sailed the ocean nearby. This bow-legged kid loved to watch them. *Maricon,* they called him. "Fairy." Too small, too weak, so two hands on the forehand. He played and played until everyone wanted to hit with him. Thirty cents an hour, then fifty cents an hour, then 10,000 hours, then 20,000 hours, then that two-handed forehand one of the greatest shots in tennis history.

Napkins, cruise liners, celebrities, dreams. Napkins at the Beverly Hills Tennis Club where Pancho reigned with his shock of white hair. On napkins he scratched out the endless patterns and possibilities of tennis physics from his unconventional Einsteinian mind. As Rod Laver said of playing Segura: *You felt like you could win, but you would start doubting yourself because his knowledge was so great.*

As only someone who came up from poverty might know in the gut, the mano a mano competition on the tennis court became, for Segura, a type of "democracy in action"—*Just me and you, baby. Doesn't matter how much money you have, or who your dad is, or if you went to Harvard, Yale or whatever. Just me and you.*

The two legendary Panchos—Gonzales and Segura—handled the WASP world differently as they toured and entertained them with tennis from the gods. Gonzales dour, bitter. Segura all smiles, jokes. They helped each other get through it all.

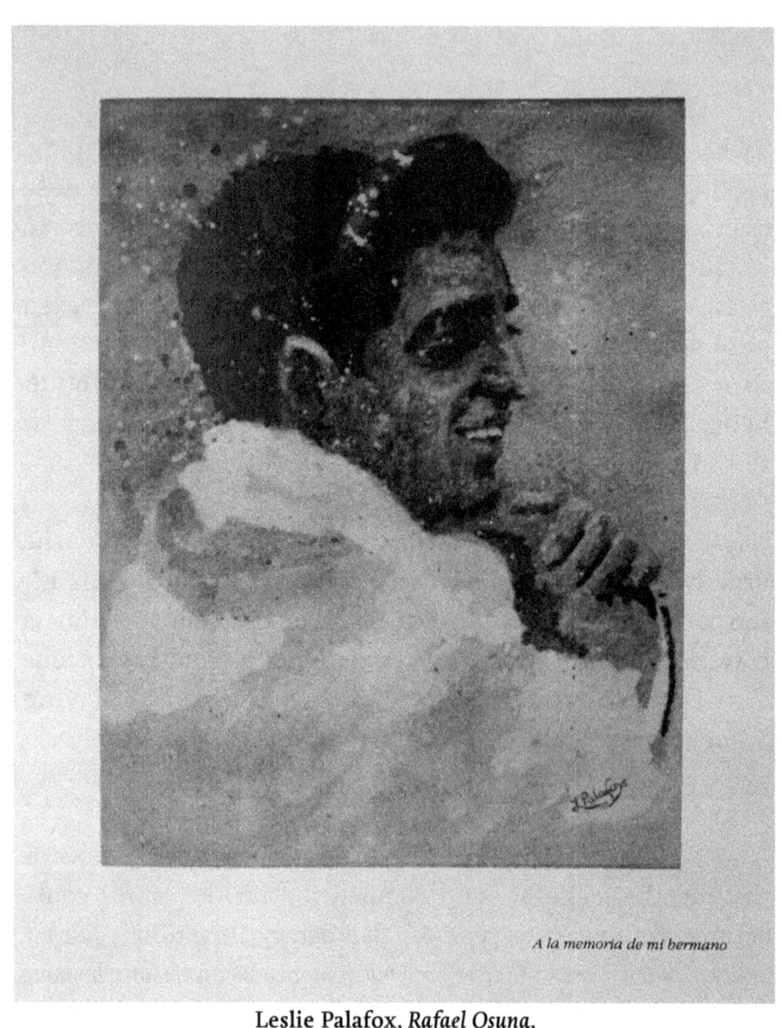

Leslie Palafox, *Rafael Osuna.*

MEXICO, RAFAEL OSUNA,

ART BY LESLIE PALAFOX
AND ENRIQUE MIGUEZ HUGUENIN

Smells of two worlds mix in the kitchen. One is boiling beans and noodle soup and chile rellenos. The other black olives, goat cheese, figs. Each day is a clock with its two hands tossing tortillas as a child appears and then another and another until Rafael is born on September 15, 1938. Trumpets and rattles (matracas) everywhere in the streets so that no one can hear his cries. Celebrations start early for September 16, the day of Mexico's independence in 1810 when Father Hidalgo delivered the *Grito (Cry) of Dolores*.

Rafael's father kept singing of how beautiful we are with our lips and eyes and our spirits of eagles and tigers and how life was elephants and diamonds and princesses and ping-pong tables. His mother would join in to pass down their legacy of the three gifts: love of books, love of music, love of sports. Life was so hot one day that little Rafael hid from everyone, so he could shave his head to cool down. That's why they called him *Pelon* ("Bald"). And soon enough everyone for miles and miles was singing and chanting and whispering and talking; *Vengan a ver al Peloncito (Come along to see Peloncito)* because at ten years old he became the youngest ever National Open Doubles Ping-Pong Champion in Mexico.

Some say he moved like a god. Some say he moved like a panther. *It's not possible to be faster than Osuna* (George Toley, his coach at USC). Rafael spent hour after hour on the ball machine after arriving at USC until suddenly, surprisingly, he's at Wimbledon in 1960 where he covers the net like a tiger—I repeat here only what the newspapers wrote—a tiger with incredible reflexes and anticipation and strategic acumen, a tiger who is always smiling and joking and in a good mood. Wimbledon doubles titles in 1960 and 1963. The US Open singles title in 1963 when he becomes the #1 player in the world.

Children mob him when he crosses the street to enter the stadium in Mexico City. *You see all of these kids, they are all sons of mine. If they don't enter, I don't.* Every time Osuna played in Mexico after that, all the children who accompanied him entered for free. Countless Davis Cup victories. Two Olympic gold medals in 1968 in Mexico City, the city of his birth.

His wife and son of five months asleep while he rises before dawn for a short, quick flight to Monterrey. Some planes never land. A racquet was placed on top of his coffin. All the headlines screamed "*Pelon.*"

Enrique Miguez Hugenin, *Rafael Osuna.*
Hugenin's statue of Rafael Osuna was first unveiled by
the president of Mexico, José Lopez Portillo.

VII: WIMBLEDON STORIES

Toupie Lowther, Photograph Postcard, c. 1900. ©AELTC/
Wimbledon Lawn Tennis Museum. Used with permission
from the Wimbledon Lawn Tennis Museum.

TOUPIE'S GHOST,

PHOTOGRAPH FROM
THE WIMBLEDON MUSEUM

Note: I first heard of Toupie Lowther from the Wimbledon Museum Twitter account, which included a photograph postcard of Toupie Lowther, on February 5, 2021: *We have been researching previously overlooked players in tennis and wanted to share this postcard of May "Toupie" Lowther with you. Wimbledon semi-finalist in 1903 and 1906, Lowther was believed to be the first openly lesbian player in the sport.*

In the piece below, I reimagine Toupie Lowther as Toupie's Ghost, still alive today, haunted by the possibility that the primary character in the controversial "first lesbian novel," Radclyffe Hall's *The Well of Loneliness*, a girl named Stephen, was partially modeled after her. (This is most likely true, though we will never know for sure.) Toupie's Ghost has plenty to say about Wimbledon as well.

TOUPIE'S GHOST

The Well of Loneliness by Radclyffe Hall was an overly sentimental novel—half-Victorian, half-Freudian—by a half-talented writer of ambition. Its protagonist is a girl named Stephen based, in part, on my life as a "queer" person. Too bad Virginia Woolf did not write it. I might not be a ghost right now. *Toupie was bitter about the book because she wanted to be known as the only invert* (Una Troubridge). Right. Just what every "queer" person wants.

We cannot touch, be touched. Not lips, but lipless. Arms without flesh. As Achilles said to Odysseus in the afterlife: *I would rather be the lowest slave in life that lord it over all the dead.* And I, Toupie Lowther, would rather be a "queer" person at the dawn of the twentieth century than Toupie's Ghost. I drove fast cars and motorbikes, fenced military men before gawking crowds. Made the semifinals at Wimbledon, too. I composed music, setting poems of Tennyson and Oscar Wilde. I helped organize and lead an all-women troupe of ambulance drivers near the front in WWI. Not even we ghosts can contemplate all that death.

Hillyard wrote of my tennis: *Her potentialities were greater than any other English lady who ever walked on court, but she was unfortunately saddled with a temperament which was so hopelessly unsuitable to lawn tennis.* If I could have focused more, ended the points more quickly, made it all parry and thrust, serve and volley. (Everyone said I would have won an Olympic gold medal in fencing if it had been an Olympic event.) If I had played in the 1970s or 80s before Venus and Serena came along, I might have transformed a legendary trio of Wimbledon champions into a quartet of serve-and-volley Amazons with multiple Wimbledon titles: Martina Navratilova (nine titles), Billie Jean King (six titles), Toupie Lowther (four titles), Margaret Court (three titles). What a dinner party that might be. I could ask Amélie "half man" (can you believe Hingis called her that?) Mauresmo to come and bring bottles of wine from her cellar. Maybe Mauresmo would be my model. Way too nervy on court, always seemed to play below her potential. Then one year she won Wimbledon.

One Wimbledon might be enough.

Stephen Gulbis, *Jana Novotna and the Duchess.*

JANA NOVOTNÁ AND KAFKA'S *THE METAMORPHOSIS,*

ART BY STEPHEN GULBIS

Leading 4-1, 40-30 in the final set for the Wimbledon title, Novotná's second serve sails halfway to the baseline. Double fault. Deuce. *Tension.* Novotná pokes a sitter forehand volley way over the baseline. Ad-out. Jana's legs imperceptibly heavier move back on a lob, her shoulder metamorphosing tightening up slowing down as it strikes the ball meekly into the bottom of the net. "It was no dream."

4-1, 4-2, 4-3. Double fault. Double fault. Double fault. Audible groans in the cathedral of tennis. Difficult to watch, difficult to worship. 4-4. *Move your feet. Do not overthink. Swing freely.* 4-4. 4-5. *Just go for your shots. Relax. Just get the ball in.* A tentative backhand slice hits the tape. "Gregor's numerous legs, which were pitifully thin compared to rest of his bulk, waved helpless before his eyes." Jana cries on the duchess's shoulder. The cameras click. The writers write. The whole world reads what is written. *I love it,* Novotná would later say. *I think about it all the time.*[*]

---

[*] Novotná won Wimbledon, her one Grand Slam singles title, five years after one of the greatest chokes in the history of sport.

Nial Smith, *Andy Murray Starring in Gladiator.*

WHAT WE DO IN WIMBLEDON FORTNIGHT,

BY SCOTT BARCLAY,
ART BY NIAL SMITH

Note: I had permission from Nial Smith to use his spoof movie poster of Andy Murray as the star of the film *Gladiator* for a piece I would write on it. After starting to write the piece, I realized that Scott Barclay, part of the podcast Murray Musings, would be a better choice to write this piece, especially since Nial, Scott, and Andy Murray are all from Scotland. This is Scott Barclay's piece inspired by Nial Smith's poster of Andy Murray.

WHAT WE DO IN WIMBLEDON FORTNIGHT

Clouds broke, breaching their way across the London sky, smokey and wispy in their sunburned paleness and altogether calming in their paced slowness.

Below, though, chaos reigned, raining down at speeds fearsome as racket hands shook and dreams shivered, wavered and quivered with goosebumps on tight ropes of potential happenings.

Breaths were being held, choking the country to a standstill stall, sun beating down and melting out across roads empty, eyes all inside watching television sets aplenty, many having left work early or abandoned it altogether for this wonder Sunday.

Over on Henman Hill, blinking, winking in the summer heat, hands sticky with ice-lollies dripping through hands clasped, gasps escaping through mouths agaping at the possibility of incoming astounding.

Right there on Wimbledon Centre, history moved, side-to-side across baselines faded, dusted, wasted away from two weeks of intensity play.

The usual hushing and shushing teetered on the edge of barely restrained desperation, arms clawing at the air around heads in fearful nervousness, pimms and strawberries scattered around feet stomping in cream running, dribbling beneath seats abandoned after every point won with a standing roaring.

Hours ticked on like this, scraping along between agony and ecstasy, bypassing all sense of usual tick-tocking, as though the significance of this day alone had reached in and meddled with the inner workings of the world clockings.

Indeed, when the final game finally came, days, weeks, months went by, seasons passed, summer drifted to winter, orange leaves falling and turning to snow carpeting the ground crunching, calendars were changed as hairs turned grey and wrinkles were set into skin once young with forlorn youth, so terribly slow did these final few points seem to go, flow as they did with a dragged out weight, that waiting for moment of greatness fulfillment, a frustrating amount of "HOW MANY OF THESE CHAMPIONSHIP POINTS IS HE GOING TO NEED TO GET IT DONE?!?!?!?!" screamed internal monologues...

And then it was over and he turned and lost himself in exhausted childhood jubilations, a yell of relief immediately drowned in the haze of the thousands that rose as one to raise him above their heads as though they themselves could in some way stake some claim to all of this immensity.

He climbed up through them, snaking his way between the back-slapping and hand-shaking, all the way up towards those that meant most, typically making sure to forget about Mum amidst all of the hugging, retracing his steps across the roof-tops of commentary booths to embrace her in a much-photo-snapped image that read "FINALLY!" with its very occurrence. Minutes later, the trophy was held in a gentle protective way, cradled as though it had a beating heart itself, beaconing its way across sports pages, front pages, all-of-the-pages like a lightning rod drizzled through with a gleeful injection of thankfulness.

A drone of a voice took us all walking through the immediate aftermath, his lifetime-achievement joy hidden under a layer of relief-stricken wonderment disguised as a shrug of noncha-lance, the tears of the years of nearly-theres ghostly distant in the memory of the watching.

The toils and the foils, the rages and turmoils, the criticism, whirlwind analysis of his emotional weaknesses, pointers from those that were never even asked, his mum strung up and blamed for apron strings no longer attached, his appear-ance mocked, laughed at, his scruffiness mocked, belittled, his talent questioned, a ruffian, a swear-box, a pest beyond all the rest, a Scot triumphant in the kingdom of British sporting greatness.

...

These were the glory days of Andy Murray summers.

Cat Lee (Colacat), *Elena Rybakina.*

ELENA RYBAKINA ON WINNING WIMBLEDON: "IT'S A FAIRY TALE,"
ART BY CAT LEE (COLACAT)

Once upon a time, a girl was born in Moscow who dreamed of winning Wimbledon. She worked hard on her serve and ground strokes, then knocked on doors of the rich and privileged for help. *Too tall, too slow, too clumsy*, the Russian prince said. *Good enough for us*, the prince of Kazakhstan said. Money was involved, a move to another country, a commitment to change flags, nationalities.

It was not foretold, but then it happens: Russia invades Ukraine. So many bombs drop that Wimbledon bans all Russians and Belarusians from the grandest of balls: Aryna, Victoria, Daria, Veronika, Ludmilla, Ekaterina... Elena, however, was allowed to play.

Three good witches waited and watched. Ash from Australia, Iga from Poland, Ons from the Islamic world.[*] Iga speaks out against Russia's invasion so close to her Polish lands. Ash retires to get married, raise a family. Ons spreads so much love throughout the world she is known as the Minister of Happiness. She will oppose Elena in the Wimbledon final. Everyone roots for Ons, for happiness, for if she wins then all girls' dreams in the Islamic world have a greater chance of coming true.

---

[*] These three good witches are: Ash Barty, the previous year's Wimbledon champion and world #1; Iga Świątek, the current #1 player in the world; Ons Jabeur, who did lose to Elena in the Wimbledon final. Ons is the most important female role model in the Islamic world.

But this is Elena's fairy tale, for she has the best serve in the world and wickedly powerful, consistent ground strokes. Some say she does not smile enough. Some say she is not pretty enough. Some say she is not marketable enough. If her dreams keep coming true, some will call her an ice queen, an assassin.

VIII: SENIORS

Remembrance Flags at the Bocage Tournament, put up by Keith Richardson, April, 2024. My Photograph.

PLAYERS PARTY IN BATON ROUGE, REMEMBRANCE FLAGS

BY KEITH RICHARDSON

Note: All the italicized lines below are from sixty- to eighty-five-year-old senior tennis players and their significant others at the annual national tournament at the Bocage Racquet Club in Baton Rouge.

Bone on bone.

Both hips replaced.

Bet this is the healthiest group of seniors in the country.

From Keith Richardson's note next to these Remembrance Flags: Earlier this year I introduced Remembrance Flags to my fellow players at a doubles tournament in Columbus, GA. The flags are patterned after the prayer flags that the people of Nepal and Tibet fly from their rooftops and temples. Names of loved ones that have passed away as well as blessings for them are inscribed on the flags and allowed to flap in the breeze. Over time the threads of the flags begin to unravel and are carried upwards to the heavens, along with the names and the blessings.

The goal of my Remembrance Flags is to recognize a fellow tennis player or coach that is no longer with us and to cause a moment of awareness, reflection and gratitude for their life and the positive impact that they had on our life and the lives of others . . . .and also, a moment of thankfulness that we are able to continue this wonderful game while recognizing that their spirit is among us while being appreciated and carried upwards.

Please feel free to add a name or names of those that have impacted your life.

We drive our RV together to tournaments, listen to books on Audible.

I play for Chile at the Worlds this year.

I love Shakespeare's plays, but I don't understand contemporary poetry when it doesn't rhyme. I much prefer prose.

Grandson getting married.

Daughter getting married.

Did you bring your guitar?

Have not seen a hunchback for years, or are you icing your shoulder?

One exercise you can do is move your shoulders back and forward like Shakira. She demonstrates. That is my husband's favorite exercise.

Wife passed away five months ago.

I worked as a secretary for forever. That's all they let women do. Got my doctorate at forty-three. Retired at sixty-seven.

So when are you going to retire, Tomas?

I'll retire at ninety-five. Win a gold ball, too, when I'm ninety-five, when most of you are no longer around.

Hey, that's my dream.

It's not just the play. It's the players, too.

Final Match Handshake at the Stagg Invitational, October 2022, Photograph by Gena Stagg.

AUTUMN AT THE STAGG INVITATIONAL,

PHOTOGRAPHY BY GENA STAGG

Mike Roberson and I shake hands after the final match. We both lost our wives this year. I am the lucky one. At sixty-five years old, two decades older than Mike, I can already check the box called a long, happy life: a blissful marriage of forty years with two beautiful daughters of intelligence and integrity, my gift of a career as a Professor of Humanities.

This handshake, this camaraderie, is repeated again and again both on and off the court between all sixteen competitors at the Stagg Invitational. We cheer for each other's good shots. We lament each other's errors. Though not much in life is free, here for one weekend everything is free: the beer, the friendships, the endless permutations of interesting, dynamic doubles points to observe from the sidelines. Doubles, partners. *That's what I miss*, I tell Mike as we watch our friends play tennis. Don't want to go through life alone.

In Gena Stagg's photograph, as in so many nineteenth-century landscape paintings, we humans are but a small part of nature. Small as we are, we are "part and parcel" of a larger whole, of the beauty and divinity of the natural world. Autumn is here. Winter is coming. Trees are losing their leaves as the sharp diagonal rays of sunlight bend closer and closer toward that

Mike Roberson and I shake hands. He is the younger, taller one. Mike won that year's championship with his partner, Mark Weil (pictured). My partner was Colin Leighton (also pictured).

certain Slant of light / Winter Afternoons, as Emily Dickinson put it. If you look closely at the bottom of the photo, you can see one or two fallen leaves. If you look closer still, you can see the various footprints we left in the clay. Soon the court will be swept, our footprints vanish.

146

Bogdan Shiptenko, *Tennis Players.*

THE NATIONAL 65 INDOORS,
ART BY BOGDAN SHIPTENKO

"I like to draw people in their habitat."
– Bogdan Shiptenko

Note: Inspired by Shiptenko's painting *Tennis Players*, I sketch tennis players at the Men's 65 National Indoors in Eden Prairie, Minnesota.

Mark Vines (#1 in the US): So much devilish spin on his lefty serve. How does he do it at 5'7"? Does he lift weights as much as his significant other, a professional weightlifter? If I lifted more weights without hurting myself, could I spin it like Vines does? No way.

Michael Tammen (#2 in the US): His game a combination of fairly flat forehands, slice backhands, solid volleys, and high-percentage serving. Everything he hits is placed with consistent precision and depth. He rarely misses and almost never hits a so-so shot his opponents might attack. I'm working hard to do all this, especially eliminating the so-so shots. It's harder than eliminating the so-so hours and days of the week. The better players can do it. That's why they're the better players.

Ross Persons (#5 in the US): Fun to watch his quick-twitch muscles cover every ball. Fun to watch his buggy-whip forehand, his deft touch from everywhere on the court. Half panache, half precision.

Stewart Jackson (#6 in the US): You can't teach height. That's what they say. Stewart's long arms and long, fluid strokes produce lots of power on every shot. Wish I could be that smooth, that powerful.

Michael Starke (#9 in the US): Short, stocky, powerful, fast... Runs down every ball and hits every shot with bodily commitment, energetic glee. Would give half my retirement savings for his two-handed backhand. Doubt he would accept it.

Juan Lopez (#9th seed): So much pop on his graceful, big forehand. He tries to hit it every chance he gets. If I tried to hit forehands as big as his, I would have to donate my elbow to science.

IX: COLLABORATIONS AND HONORED GUESTS

Katie Podracky, *Mark Mathabane*.

KAFFIR BOY, MARK MATHABANE (THE BEST TENNIS STORY I KNOW),

ART BY KATIE PODRACKY

Apartheid means separation. Separation means hate. Kaffir Boy lives in an all-black ghetto of one square mile, 200,000 people. No running water, electricity, or paved roads. You had to put up with so much shit no outsider would believe it. Mother hides in a ditch most mornings. Never know when the police might come. You need a pass for a family to live together. You need a pass to work. You need a pass to flit like a servile, unseen ghost anywhere in the white man's world. Authorities dole out passes in unfathomable ways. Wait forever in line on multiple days with multiple papers in hand, never knowing if you have the right ones. If you can't get a pass to work, you can be arrested for being unemployed.

When Arthur Ashe plays a tournament in South Africa, he tells white men what he thinks and believes without apology. If Arthur Ashe had been black in South Africa, he would have hanged himself in prison. That's what Kaffir Boy tells a friend. Black activists often hung themselves in prison using shoelaces. That's what the authorities said. Kaffir Boy and his friend agree: *we call it cold-blooded murder.*

Kaffir Boy falls in love with books. Kaffir Boy falls in love with tennis. Somehow he hits tennis balls with 1972 US and

Wimbledon champion Stan Smith, who helps him get a tennis scholarship to America. While in college, Mark Mathabane writes *Kaffir Boy*, the story of his life growing up in South Africa under apartheid. *Kaffir Boy* becomes a bestseller. It's the best book I know about apartheid. Not sure I know a better tennis story.

Mark on tennis: Tennis literally saved my life. It was the catalyst for the tough choices I had to make en route to America: to defy gangs, to focus on school despite the Dickensian conditions of black education, to learn English, my fifth language, and stop hating white people for apartheid and judge them as individuals, by their deeds. This led to books and tennis and eventually to meeting Stan. Finally, what tennis empowered me to achieve is nothing short of miraculous. I was able, in one generation, to go from sleeping on pieces of cardboard in a shack without running water or electricity, hunting for food at garbage dumps, and being dragged to school by my illiterate mother to save me from the dead-end life of gangs as the first of her seven children—to graduating with honors from an American college, writing several books, including two bestsellers, serving as a White House Fellow in 1996, bringing the rest of my family to America and educating my six siblings, and seeing my three children, who were inspired by Kaffir Boy's story, all graduate from Princeton.

Mark on Alexandra (aka Alex): Alex is only ten miles from Kempton Park, where Roger Federer's mom grew up. Nelson Mandela, a tennis player and fan who keenly followed Ashe's exploits (while serving life imprisoned on Robben Island), lived in Alex in 1940, several blocks from the shack where I was born. In *Long Walk to Freedom*, Mandela fondly reminisces about the residents' sense of community despite being mired in desperate poverty. Sadly, that poverty hasn't been alleviated, despite Alexandra's key role in the liberation struggle and cultural history of the country and Southern Africa. You may want to check out its Wikipedia list of Notable Residents, which includes the poet Mongane Wally Serote, jazz trumpeter Hugh Masekela, Samora Machel, the first president of an Independent Mozambique, and Hastings Banda, President of Malawi.

Note on *Kaffir Boy*: "Kaffir" is now classified as hate speech. The K-word in South Africa is roughly equivalent to the N-word in America. *Kaffir Boy*, which won a Christopher Award for inspiring hope, has been one of the most popular books in America's public schools since its publication in 1987, despite nationwide efforts to ban it as "pornography." Teachers use it to primarily inspire students, especially from marginalized communities, to never give up on their dreams, despite the obstacles in their way.

Nial Smith, *David Hall.*

DAVID HALL'S GOLDEN SOCKS,
ART BY NIAL SMITH

"This party was a one-off. To win a gold medal in a Paralympics not only in my home country, but actually in the city of my birth where I lived, would never happen again."
          – David Hall

The gold medal's been in my sock drawer for twenty years, so whenever I get socks I relive the day, its unrelenting pressure, the 10,000-plus fans waving Aussie flags, the muscle-bound arms of the American Stevie Welch, my archrival, pushing his wheelchair like a madman...

I press harder and harder, litter the first set with errors, and lose it in a tiebreaker. When I go down early in the second, I start sneaking into the net, totally against my nature, trying anything to change the dynamics. At 5-4 in the second, my set point, I hit a sweet backhand up the line, the American grunting, trying to track it down, the crowd beginning to roar through the windy conditions that always seem to blow through the suburbs of Sydney, my birthplace, my home... The umpire calls out the score, but no one can hear. The crowd was all in, and so was I.

At 5-2 up in the third, at the change of ends, the emotions start to bubble up. I have to stay calm, play a solid game. When the American hits a final forehand long, the tears start to run down my face. Tears of relief and dreams and obstacles and triumph as the Australian flag is raised and the national anthem sung; as the three medalists do a lap of the court in front of 10,000 fans; as I do another lap alone, holding aloft an Australian flag somebody in the crowd had given me.

I tell this story to another small crowd before me with a smile on my face. I know someone wants to ask: *Why does a man without feet need socks?* My stumps get cold, I tell them.

Socks and medals, strange bedfellows.

This piece was co-written by David Hall and David Linebarger.

Coach Cox and Blake Strode together at the US Open.
Photo courtesy of Robert Cox.

WHAT A UNIVERSITY TENNIS COACH LEARNS FROM HIS PLAYERS,

BY ROBERT COX (HEAD COACH AT UNIVERSITY OF ARKANSAS, 1987-2013)

What I learned from Blake Strode: Recruits like Blake do not come around very often. He was the complete package: smarts, natural talent, high junior rankings, speed, and a high tennis IQ. For four years, Blake played high in the lineup earning All American honors, leading his team to a top-fifteen ranking, reaching the men's singles NCAA semifinals. But from my perspective, his greatest accomplishment was teaching me about Black History in America and race relations. Blake had a set of Black History flash cards that he would bring on team trips and he would quiz me in the team van. My knowledge of Black History in America was very limited and my stock answers to his quizzes were limited to two answers: Martin Luther King and Rosa Parks. Throughout Blake's four years at Arkansas, he educated me about the struggles/injustices Blacks faced in America against "The Man." I am so grateful for Blake's time here at Arkansas and all that he taught me. The view of the world that I now possess, thanks to Blake, is much more important to me than any win he gave me on the court. When I hear on the news or read an article about race relations/injustices/struggles in America, I look at it differently because I was lucky enough to coach Blake for four years. After playing on tour and graduating from Harvard Law School, Blake became the Executive Director of Arch City Defenders in St. Louis. My favorite quote from Blake is about attorneys serving people: *The vast majority of legal work is for high-paying corporations or high-net-worth individual clients. In my view, the need is greatest among low-income, working-class, poor and homeless individuals.*

What I learned from Oskar Johansson: Oskar arrived on campus with confidence. He had this inner self-belief, but he was also "stubborn." If Oskar did not believe in what I was coaching, there was almost no chance he would consider incorporating it into his tennis personality. As a coach, I did not enjoy coaching Oskar for the first year and a half. He not only questioned my coaching, but he did so many times in front of the team. After three semesters, though, I realized that by having him on the team, he was making me a better coach. I had to make sure I could defend my coaching philosophy in all areas of the program. Oskar also slowly opened up to new ideas and thought processes over time. He began to look at tennis and life through a different lens and realized he was equipped to play number one for an SEC top-twenty team. He ascended in the national rankings, ultimately becoming #1 in the NCAA/ITA rankings.

My proudest moment with Oskar was on Senior Day. Oskar's parents had traveled from Malmo, Sweden, to Fayetteville for the first time in his four years as a student-athlete to watch their son play in a Razorback uniform. Oskar quickly fell behind his opponent due to his tight play, playing as the #1-ranked player in the country, playing on center court, and wanting to impress his parents. I felt badly for Oskar as I had grown to love this young man. Then out of nowhere a rainstorm quickly descended on the outdoor courts, halting the dual match with Auburn in the lead 2-1 and in front of the remaining four matches. Due to this rainstorm, the match was moved to the intimate indoor courts of the Dills Center, awarding Oskar and his Razorback teammates a fresh start. Led by Oskar's brilliant play, the Razorbacks turned the tables and stubbornly, confidently, and enthusiastically defeated the Tigers 4-2. During Oskar's match, I would steal a look into the crowd and find Oskar's dad smiling and clapping for his son, who was making him so proud in this courageous comeback. When Oskar's teammate Aleksey Bubis clinched the match, I quickly scanned the facility and found Oskar—pointed my finger at him—locked eyes with him—and felt his acceptance. Oskar remains to this day, twenty years after that Senior Day one of my closest friends.

Note: This piece came about when I asked Coach Cox if I could get his impressions of five or six of his favorite players for a piece I would write. He sent me one, then another. I realized, then, that this should be a piece he should write in his own voice. This is that piece.

Andy Ramirez, *The Millers.*

STRING THERAPY,

BY JIMMY MILLER,
ART BY ANDY RAMIREZ

Before my father died when I was twelve, he taught me to play tennis and string racquets. Forty-seven years and some 80,000 racquets later, I can still remember the smell of heated wood after quickly pulling a small piece of spare string through the rough holes of a wooden racket. "Burning them out," we called it, the friction smoothing the edges, before we started to string. I can still remember the feel of mounting the racquet and easing down the weighted foot pedal on Dad's prized Serrano stringing machine. *Straighten the strings, Jimmy, always,* he would patiently remind me. Out in the front of the tennis shop we would carefully brush thick, golden shellac onto the natural gut strings, then watch it glisten in the summer sun. Customers today often comment that stringing looks therapeutic. I nod and smile. If they ask how I learned, I tell them about my dad.

This drawing of the Millers, of me and my dad, was a surprise gift from Andy Ramirez, a close friend and doubles partner who owned a small ad agency down the street from where I was going to school at Santa Clara University. One day Andy asked if he could borrow a couple of tennis photos of me and my dad, saying he wanted to work on rebuilding his drawing skills. Andy never knew my father, yet he knew how much my father meant to me.

The last string straightened, I handed the racquet over to the customer. They can't wait to play. I feel renewed. Andy used to tell me that with each string job, I was restringing a soul.

Maybe each racquet I string is an unspoken thank-you to my father for giving me his love of tennis, the art of racquet stringing. Another racquet finished. I hand it over. *Restringing a soul*, Andy said. *My own*, I think, and become whole again.

Note on the origin of this piece: This piece started when I saw Jimmy Miller post a drawing of the Millers, of him and his father, on Twitter. Sensing a great story about friends giving gifts of art and of fathers passing down traditions (such as tennis), I asked Jimmy if I might use this artwork for a piece of writing. As I began to explore this work and emailed back and forth with Jimmy about it, I soon realized that he had a beautiful piece of writing on everything this drawing might mean. This is that writing.

Andy Ramirez, who created the artwork of the Millers, graduated from San Jose State University with a degree in art. A doubles partner and tennis buddy of Jimmy's, Andy was the owner and Creative Director of Ramirez & Associates Advertising Agency for over thirty years.

Michael Newberry, *Self-Portrait.*

TENNIS OR ART:
A SELF-PORTRAIT,

ART AND WRITING
BY MICHAEL NEWBERRY

I was twenty and holed up in a hotel room in Frankfurt, Germany, contemplating my future. I was torn between two really good career options: to continue being a pro tennis player (I was beating guys top 100 in the world) or give everything I had to my art. The week involved a tremendous amount of self-assessment, a ruthless look at my skill sets, my strengths, weaknesses in both fields. Tennis had to be decided upon quickly; I was the age to commit, as a pro career is generally from then to thirty-two. With my art, on the other hand, I was still a student, and normally great artists mature around their late twenties to early thirties. But the rub there is that artists have to put in between ten to 20,000 hours before their art starts to gel.

One suggestive indication that I had already chosen was that instead of tennis training that week, I just read and drew in my hotel room. There was a tournament the next week, and I chose not to prepare for it. The mental gymnastics I went through was draining and a bit painful. You can see that in the eyes of this self-portrait. I felt tremendous urgency to clear my brain with a clear choice and get it done with. So I kept hashing through every pro and con I could think of: would I ever have a great backhand drive? Did I accomplish everything in art I tried? Did I want a traveling tennis life and to see the world? Or was painting in a dumpy studio more exalting? Could I cheat it and do tennis now and art later?

Another important consideration is that an art life/career is forever—an artist can keep evolving until the day they die. Tennis has its specific physical limitations; it is downhill from one's thirties.

I am thankful that the young me had the foresight, gumption, psychological savvy, and introspection to make the choice to be an artist. I have loved and love every second of living the art life; every obstacle was/is a delicious challenge to grow and flourish. In all that time I only recall having one moment of regret. I was painting *Woman in Blue*—I was twenty, it was late at night, and I was pushing my limits. It was in Holland, wintertime, and hail was ferociously beating at the window-panes like aggressive and anxious bats. For a few seconds I thought I could be playing tennis in the south of France, or touring Australia, warm and dry playing on a magnificent center court. Then I saw something I could tweak in the painting, and I thought: *hell no, I don't want to be hitting a ball somewhere—I am bringing this woman to life; there is no other place in the universe I would rather be.*

(The excerpts above are from Michael Newberry's "Early Work, Self-Portrait 1977.")

X: AUSSIES AND BODY PARTS, MARK SHORTER'S PAINTINGS

What follows is a collaborative dialogue of art and words on famous Australian tennis players with Mark Shorter, the endlessly innovative Australian artist and head of sculpture at the University of Melbourne. My thanks to Gertrude Contemporary, the leading incubator of contemporary art in Australia, for hooking us up.

Mark Shorter, *Margaret*.

MARGARET COURT'S NECK

Margaret Court, the Aussie Amazon, did sprints in the sand and lifted weights when workouts for "ladies" were a dirty word. On first encountering her, Martina Navratilova said what so many women felt: *Margaret amazed me with her size and strength.* Nicknamed "The Arm" for her power overhead (the serve, the smash) and incredible reach on court, Margaret becomes "The Neck" in Shorter's portrait. Well, Margaret has certainly stuck her neck out with her attacks on Martina Navratilova, Billie Jean King, and the entire LGBTQ community. One way to read Shorter's lovingly?—accusingly?—aggressively?—bitterly?—righteously?—tenderly?—rendered painting of gloriously thick purples and browns and yellows is within the tradition of still-life painting. The fruit, once ripe, is rotting. The flesh, once muscled, sags. Margaret's ideas, once societal truisms, need to be taken out to the trash.

I do not know which to prefer—the thick, sagging, glory/antiglory of Margaret's neck, or the more rigidly structured clash of colors in Margaret's face. Eyes cut off, ears cut off, forehead (read: brain) lobotomized. Margaret's implacable, unseeing face suggests something insidious for the LGBTQ community that all "others" know well: *I do not see you. I do not hear you. I do not know/consider your reality.*

When Bobby Riggs brought her roses before humiliating her in the Mother's Day Massacre (6-2, 6-1) before fifty million television viewers, Court curtsied before playing the most passive, disappointing match of her life. (*She, curtsied!* Billic Jean King would later write in disbelief.) Four months later,

King crushed Riggs in the Battle of the Sexes. Yet in her great rivalry with Billie Jean, Margaret Court was the better player: a 22-10 head-to-head advantage and 4-1 in Grand Slams. The record books, in fact, sing hymns of praise to Margaret Court. Calendar Grand Slam in 1970. First (and only) mother to be ranked #1. Twenty-four Grand Slam singles titles, the all-time record. Shorter's portrait of Court invites us—shouts at us—to consider the rest.

Mark Shorter, *Lew.*

LEW HOAD'S NOSE

Greek Tragedy #1: That something within everyone like Achilles' heel is fated and waiting to fail. For Lew Hoad it was his back.

Greek Tragedy #2: What being born a decade too soon might mean. His homeland (Australia) would exile him, history forget him[*] (slightly overstated but not by much).

In Medias Res: Pills swallowed, shots taken, drink. Difficult, sometimes impossible, to tie his shoes. Driving all night in uncomfortable cars that first year as a pro with Pancho Gonzalez: *Lew Hoad the only guy who, if I were playing my best tennis, could still beat me.*

Earlier: Lew Hoad a celebrity in 1950s' black-and-white: politicians getting wet in locker room showers to shake his hand, tram drivers stopping trains to shout out scores from his Davis Cup matches.

Later: Richard Burton drunk on Shakespeare while Cleopatra sleeps inside the Campo de Tenis in Spain, the house that Lew Hoad built. The great questions of life are decided there. How much cognac, Cointreau should we put in the sangria? What's that riff Stan Getz smokes on the sax?

---

[*] What turning pro meant: 1) You could not play for your country, so your country (Australia) disowned you. 2) You could not play Wimbledon or any of the Grand Slams, so the future will never quite be able to count or recount what happened when you walked the earth.

Throughout: Lew's bedroom eyes—what Jenny, his wife, called them. Lew a forty-year lover of great intensity, his body like a Greek or Roman statue.

Posters of Lew Hoad on walls of memories inside a young tennis player's artistic mind: *I've finally finished my picture of Lew. I don't know why it took so long. Perhaps it's because he was so enigmatic. In the pictures I studied of him he was so graceful, statuesque, classic. That's why I painted his nose like I was staring up at a Greek god* (Mark Shorter). Lew's nose looks like it belongs on Mt. Rushmore, his nose both idealized Greek Classical and Roman Realistic. As Michael Taylor writes in *Rembrandt's Nose: Of Flesh & Spirit in the Master's Portraits*, Rembrandt's noses often *serve to focus the viewer's attention upon, and to dramatize, the division between a flood of light—an overwhelming clarity—and a brooding duskiness.* In Mark Shorter's painting, the drama is between this world of flesh-muscle-bone-sculpture and the blue sky above us, whatever its transcendent beauty means. For me, at least, Lew Hoad lives on in both worlds as a tennis player: not a grinder but glorious, his strong wrists and arms hitting incredible winners from any position on the court. What he lacked was shot selection, discipline, percentages...

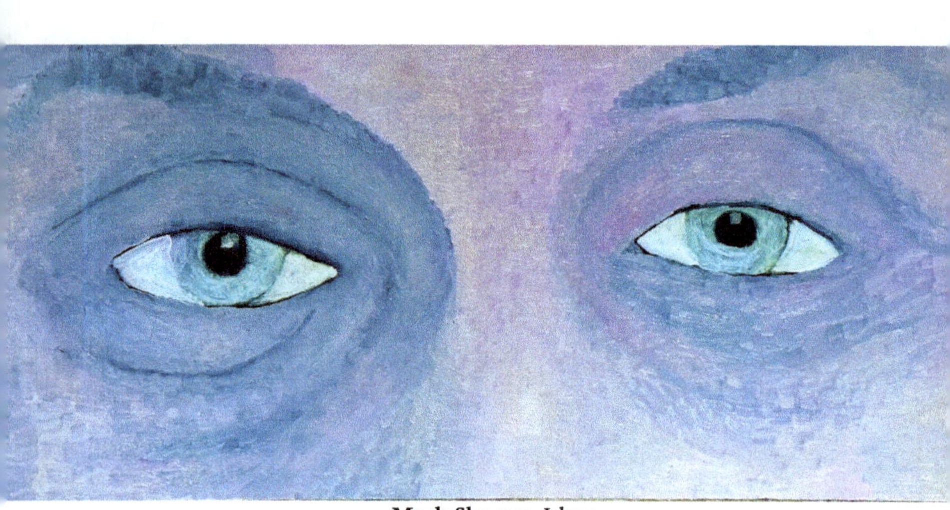

Mark Shorter, *Jelena*.

JELENA DOKIC'S EYES

In junior tournaments, Jelena is ruthless, unemotional. She even cheats on line calls to avoid her father's beatings. He smacks her in the head with shoes, punches her in the stomach. He wraps her many wounds in words of love/ambition: *prostitute, whore, hopeless, worthless...* Jelena's only twelve, keeps rising in the rankings. Fear of punishment works. *When I painted this work, I thought a lot about her relationship to the game and her father. I was interested in the way she stared back, waiting to receive the ball, waiting to receive a question at a press conference, etc.* (Mark Shorter). Like Jimmy Connors at the US Open, the 187th-ranked Jelena is rocking the stadium in a string of upsets on her way to the quarterfinals at the 2009 Aussie Open after years of on-court and off-court struggles. After another big upset of a highly ranked opponent, she confesses on court, *I've been to hell and back.*

Every day Sarah watched Isaac and Abraham from the window as they went down the valley...[*] At thirteen, fourteen, fifteen, sixteen, Jelena is yelled at and whipped, kicked and hit like a mistreated animal. *Abraham climbed Mt. Moriah...* Jelena Dokic only seventeen, and in the semifinals of Wimbledon. *But when Isaac saw Abraham's face again, it had changed: His face was wild. His whole being was sheer terror.* Listening in the car to Jelena's no-holds-barred autobiography, *Unbreakable,* I lift my hands from the steering wheel to kill her father, to kill all those fathers who deserve to be killed. Then I gather myself and finish the drive home.

---

[*] All the words in the second paragraph in italics are from Kierkegaard's Fear and Trembling and his retelling of the Isaac and Abraham story.

After losing in the semifinals at Wimbledon in 2001, Jelena's father abandons her in the clubhouse. She has nowhere to go, nowhere to sleep. History's eyes raise questions. Bodies hit the ball back with all their might.

182

Mark Shorter, *Rod.*

ROD LAVER'S EAR

Mark on his painting: *For this painting I focused on his ear because it is such an intimate space. It is where whispers are spoken. It is the site of the annunciation. It is a space of vulnerability. Rod Laver's iconic stature in the world of tennis is well established. And for those of us who never saw him play this iconic status becomes even more elevated. In a way we access his legend through players that acknowledge his legacy explicitly in their game. Like Roger Federer. When we watch Federer are we also watching Laver in a strange twice- or three-times-removed way?*

WHY THE TENNIS GODS MADE ROD LAVER

After Paul Harvey's "So God Made a Farmer"

The tennis gods looked down on the mess they had made: *We need someone so physically unremarkable and mentally unassuming no one could believe the tennis player he would become.* So the tennis gods made Rod Laver.

We need someone who will drive for endless miles on the edge of sleep like truckers do, play tennis in risky conditions in the spotlight of dim arenas. We need someone willing to get the snot beat out of him for two straight years by Lew Hoad and Ken Rosewall, knowing you play the best to become the best, that you learn more from losses, not wins. So the tennis gods made Rod Laver.

Laver listened to whispers he had dirtied the sport, had shamed himself, by turning pro. He was banned from all the

Grand Slams, banned from representing Australia in international competition. Laver listened to the tennis gods whisper.

We were witnesses at the dawning of something original, new (did we help create it?): how he could hold every shot to the last possible moment before changing its spin or direction or pace, how he could play serve and volley and hit wicked topspin passing shots, how he who could hit all sorts of lobs—defensive, offensive, slice, topspin—and get back as quick as anyone to finish a point with an inside-out lefty smash.

Federer wept.

Laver hands Roger Federer the championship trophy after the 2006 Australian Open in Rod Laver Arena. *I want to thank Rod Laver,* Federer begins.

Note: Laver won the Calendar Grand Slam in 1962 as the best amateur player in the world, then won the Calendar Grand Slam a second time in 1969 as the best tennis player in the world.

Mark Shorter, *Pat.*

PAT CASH'S LEGS

Mark on his painting: *Pat Cash occupies a special place in my young tennis heart. He was someone we all aspired to in Australia. At the junior tournaments we all wore the chequered headband and everyone leapt at the ball just that little bit harder, mimicking Cash's athleticism. This was the thing that most captivated me: the physical way he played the game. The way he held the court with his body. All quarters covered like some prowling cat.*

When I first saw Mark's painting, I was floored. Cash's tree-trunk legs their geography aboriginal lush rainforest primordial green-yellow strength roots lions birds and five-necked guitars wearing white checkered headbands leaping overhead. Cash's headband a tribute to Rick Nielsen, the virtuoso lead guitarist of Cheap Trick, rockin' the intro to "Ain't That a Shame," fingers flying higher and faster ecstasy elemental Cezanne-like brushstrokes thick varied leaves and ferns. Then blinding white light. Pat Cash's shorts. Wimbledon's dress codes. Pastoral, pristine grass. How many tennis players in the eighties—Pat, John, Vitas, Mats—dreamed of exchanging their tennis racquets for electric guitars?

Jack Black was right. The best way to stick it to the man is rock 'n' roll. Wimbledon was the man in 1987 when Cash won his only Grand Slam title with consistent volleying, strong serving, superb athleticism, enough good returns. Like the rock guitarist he wanted to be, Cash broke with tradition and climbed into the crowd. Royalty was aghast. Tennis celebrations would never be the same. Have a few beers. Get out your racquets. Plug in AC/DC, the Stones.

Mark Shorter, *Leslie*.

LESLIE TURNER BOWERY: HAND SCULPTURES

Mark on his paintings: *What I found captivating about Leslie Turner was the way she unconsciously produced these shapes with her hands when she hit the ball. They are so beautiful to me. In a way they are like reifications of her concentration. Hand sculptures! And as sculptures they are forms that reflect her capacity to focus and hold time so as to direct her energy into each ball, which contributes to each point, and to each game, and to each match. I like to think that throughout her career she produced millions of these hand sculptures.*

HAND SCULPTURES

Leslie Turner Bowery hitting a ground stroke, fingers elegantly splayed in her non-racquet hand. In tennis the off-hand's balance, ballet. Not primary, but partner. Unnoticed, noticed. A viola in symphonies. A viola in string quartets.

I read books and books about hands: visionaries, carpenters, lovers, musicians. Pianists, violinists, classical guitarists—the instrument I played—the right hand's combination of flesh and fingernail touching just right each vibratory string while the left hand stretched mind's desired precision up and down the neck's fretboard in endless combinations. Hand sculptures! Mind making hand doing something to be done as well as possible. Leslie Turner did it with her elegant ground strokes, her control of spin and power and angle and depth, her two French Open titles on clay, her eleven Grand Slam doubles championships, her seven victories over Margaret Court.

Mark Shorter, *Ash*.

ASH BARTY AND EVONNE GOOLAGONG

Mark Shorter: *For my next painting I wanted to paint both Ash Barty and Evonne Goolagong in tandem (not in the same canvas but side by side). In light of Barty's Wimbledon win it felt right. Painting them together opens up a consideration of time and experience. How might events be understood as moments that extend and overlap rather than as sequences positioned in a past/present and future? Painting as a process is one way for such ideas to be considered because of the way it can slow down an image. I'm looking forward to seeing what emerges in this experience.*

ASH BARTY'S FIST

When I was painting Ash, Mark Shorter writes, I focused on the fist pump: that singular moment of triumph that is savored after winning a tough point. I like the way she brings that moment in. Holds it and harnesses that experience of the point.

Ash hated traveling to tournaments. That's why she quit tennis as a top junior prospect. That's why she quit the second time when she was just twenty-five and the #1 player in the world. Only one in a million would do that. Ash's breakthrough came when she finally learned to respect her opponents: their tennis games, their life stories, their dreams, their demons.

Ash asks Evonne Goolagong if she might pay tribute to her scalloped-hem dress on the fiftieth anniversary of her first Wimbledon title. Evonne is Wiradjuri, Ash Ngarigo…

194

Mark Shorter, *Evonne*.

EVONNE GOOLAGONG

Note: Shortly after my wife of forty years passed away, I received an unexpected gift in the mail from Australia. A few days after, I received the following explanatory email from Mark. It would be the final painting we would work on together.

Mark's Email, April 18, 2022: I wanted to reveal to you when the painting had arrived that it was a picture of Evonne Goolagong Cawley's hand holding the ball while hitting a shot. As we had exchanged previously, I had been fascinated by the hand that the mind was not focused on and so pursued painting Evonne in this manner. I felt it opened up the reading of the painting. As the mind itself is not focused on this hand, so this hand can lead us to beyond the illustrative.

I also wanted to say that I painted this painting outside of the close-ups of Australian tennis players. I have been struggling to paint Evonne so I thought it would be nice to paint her hand with the intention above and to post it knowing it was where our exchange had first begun and that it had a deep resonance.

With respect to painting Evonne, I am still working on this painting. A friend of mine, Kieryn, suggested that maybe I had been looking in the wrong place to capture the Evonne close-up. He suggested that it was her lightness of feet that came through in those images of her hitting the ball. I had to agree and so have been letting this image of her feet rising while hitting the ball sit in my imagination and brew.

EVONNE GOOLAGONG

Wiradjuri Cummeragunga Yota Yota Goolagong the dreaming rock art walkabout Goolagong *a feathery style* (Chris Evert) not serve and volley but *Serve and Saunter* (Martina Navratilova) Goolagong moved so gracefully distracted opponents would watch Goolagong our first *Aborigine to become champion* Goolagong first racquet the side of a fruit crate Goolagong etched in the dirt the number of times she hit the ball Goolagong we should not romanticize the most graceful mover and poetic athlete in tennis history Goolagong history warns us not to romanticize the indigenous the Aboriginal Goolagong Quinkamassacres assimilation immigration destruction Goolagong dreaming *white man's bullets ripping through the flesh of my ancestors* Goolagong means *tall trees near still water* Wiradjuri word *gulagallang* means something like *a big mob* Goolagong walkabout a loss of concentration that's what the commentators said Goolagong walkabout a nomadic tradition, *a cleansing of the spirit by moving to another place for a time* after many years Goolagong: *I believe the way I played the game reflected a calmness, a serenity of spirit which I now equate with being Aboriginal.*

MARIA SHARAPOVA,
ART BY TOM LOHNER

Sharapova painted as a relentless puppet machine in a femme fatale nightmare. *Surreal but real* is how Lohner describes his art. Sharapova painted the moment before she cracks a serve, the background paint dripping upward in anticipatory dread. Sharapova's cool assassin's bullets accompanied by 100-decibel shrieks and screams. Some fans complain, but they all come out to watch this tall, leggy Russian-American with a six-page spread in the *Sports Illustrated Swimsuit Issue*. Year after year, more endorsement money than any female athlete on Earth. But not easy being blonde, a bombshell. Not easy getting spanked by Serena Williams eighteen straight times for twelve straight years—ouch! ouch! ouch! ouch!—after Sharapova beat her at Wimbledon and the WTA finals in 2004. "During games of special importance you can increase your Mildronate [the trade name for Meldonium] dose to 3-4 pills (1 hr before the match)." How to win matches, how to look good, all the while selling products, the female self. *I shop, therefore I am*, writes feminist artist Barbara Kruger. Female identity, how it's constructed...

Joan LeMay, *Vitas Gerulaitis.* Joan's portrait first appeared in *Racquet Magazine*, Issue 11.

VITAS GERULAITIS: IN MEMORIAM,

ART BY JOAN LEMAY

Vitas practiced his weaknesses for hours on end: the second serve, cocaine. This week's writing challenge: *describe his hair.* The result, a failure: lion locks Lithuanian *in its riding of the rolling level underneath it* within it surfers girls waves omg *dapple-dawn-drawn Falcon*[*] I want to touch it see it live again please live please Epitaph: **Generous.** Always picked up the tab, always there for others. *Vitas the first one I recall who gave free racquets to children* (Billie Jean King). Epitaph: **Sui Generis.** When he finally beat Jimmy Connors, he deadpanned, *No one beats Vitas Gerulaitis seventeen times in a row.* Epitaph: **Tennis Player.** Vitas trained as hard as anyone, hitting balls with the ultra-patient Borg for hours. For those who saw it, their Wimbledon five-set semifinal was a classic of shot-making, court coverage, drama, sportsmanship. And that halo of tennis balls in Joan LeMay's painting? A divine aura? A dizziness or dazedness from partying too much? A constellation of stars—read: celebrities who flocked around Vitas as the life of the party? Sainthood? Vitas was a saint; Vitas was no saint. Tennis sainthood? Let's canonize him here. Epitaph: **Beloved.** Everyone, I mean everyone, loved Vitas, including champions as different as Borg, Connors, Evert, McEnroe, Sampras... After a brutal loss, Pete Sampras remembers being spent and alone in the locker room when someone unexpectedly walked in: *Vitas unlaces my shoes, puts a dry shirt on me, puts my racquets away.* A faulty pool heater, carbon monoxide, forty years old.

---

[*] The lines in italics, with slight changes, are from Gerard Manly Hopkins's poem, "The Windhover."

Caspar Ruud as Viking, Photography by David Yarrow.

DAVID YARROW'S BEASTS: SHARKS, BEARS, AND CASPER RUUD

Yarrow's Beasts: Spend thirty hours in the water with sharks. Follow polar bears from place to place. Study their habitat, their ways. Find the best place in the world to photograph them. All you need is black and white. The sublime of nature. Not God's smiling flowers or psychedelic sunsets, but nature red in tooth and claw. Immersion. Intimacy. Two words that Yarrow lives by. Get as close or closer than Caravaggio did when he painted Christ so that you're there in the tomb when the body's laid in it. Yarrow's first big photo was a shark fully engaged in a moment of predatory joy. Extraordinary close-ups of bears and bison and lions followed where the camera lens *looks two ways,*[*] both into the eyes of the predator and into our own momentary terror of Darwinian truth. Kill or be killed. Eat or be eaten. Immersion. Intimacy. Nature.

Casper Ruud as Viking: Black and white. Clouds and crags. Gudvangen, Norway. Vikings emerge from the water's shadowy past of terror, half-human creatures that care little for what we or our civilization think. Ruud's animal skin cannot conceal a chiseled chest and face, a perfectly muscled core. The Vikings practiced sports with rocks and stones. Ruud would have beaten them all with that forehand of his thrown at 4,000 rpm with the accuracy and determination that could kill a man. Tennis is *cock-fighting for civilized people.* No blood is shed, but the practice of war is the same. The forehand's the sword. The backhand's the shield.

---

[*] Yarrow's favorite quote from Ansel Adams.

Nial Smith, *Shingo Kunieda.*

SHINGO KUNIEDA, "KAMI,"
ART BY NIAL SMITH

Questions: How Japanese is this striking poster from the Scottish designer, Nial Smith? How Japanese is this writing?

Let's talk Zen. Let's talk tennis. Shingo as Samurai warrior elite Zen mind/no-mind so quiet it becomes one with the object of its attention. The body-sword-mind-racquet moves quickly, clearly, with a subtle power not unlike that of Ken Rosewall's legendary sliced backhand: *soft yet hard, power yet touch, yin and yang.* Tennis as art, Shingo's sword/racquet a Zen calligrapher's brush whose swift sweep of motion half-creates half-energizes the Japanese script above his head: "*Courage,*" "*Bravery.*"

Naomi Osaka could never be depicted in such a Japanese way! a friend complained. We gathered word salads in the gardens of social media while watching Naomi smack some balls: *warrior kawaii rapper ballet Haitian emoji* **screaming forehand winners down the line** *LOL #1 shy island power multi-ethnic Pokémon hip* **119 mph serve.**

Shingo's return of serve, the shot I love most from history's greatest male wheelchair player. Think Agassi, Connors. Think all-out aggression, exquisite timing, add Shingo rolling forward faster further than any able-bodied player before slashing topspin rippers from both wings. Shingo's a great mover, too, like all the big four: Murray, Djokovic, Nadal, Federer. Can your eyes register the speed of Shingo's reverse spin moves from defensive positions to recover back into the court? Mine cannot.

No one knew the answer. *How many gods in Japan?* The Japanese guest speaker started to count them off for my daughter's fourth-grade class: *paper god, rice god, god of school and learning, sun god, god of water, god of music, Mt. Fuji... Infinity,* he finally said. *Do you know that number? These are the gods of the Shinto religion.* I would add Shingo God, too, God or "kami" best translated as something like a "sacred presence" of power or beauty that invokes in us a feeling of awe. Naomi kami, too. Why not? Wash your hands, clap twice, bow.

Jeffrey Sparr, *Beat Depression*. Photograph of Jeff holding his painting, *Beat Depression*, inspired by the life of Cliff Richey.

CLIFF RICHEY, JEFFREY SPARR, AND THE BELLY OF THE WHALE

You're a frigging protozoan sitting there. You're fixing to drown.[*] In the catacombs of early Christian art, the Jonah story lingers, pointing to an extensive oral history of dramatic tellings and retellings. *You start reaching pain levels you didn't think were there. Heaviness descending over you. It sits on you.* The whale crudely drawn on catacomb walls, Jonah allegorically seen as Christ, at first, then the Christian believer, delivered from death. Perfect for all the dead lying buried around. *I put black trash bags over the windows. I sealed the edges with tape. My mind became dark; and then darker; and then darker still.*

For Cliff Richey, the belly of the whale has a contemporary name: clinical depression. How to confront such darkness, despair? As Cliff Richey details throughout his story, one way is to analyze all our own strengths and weaknesses and never stop fighting, never give in. Another way is to emphasize faith, another meditation, another science with its endless ways of addressing this or that chemical imbalance. I have fallen in love with the image of Jeffrey Sparr holding up his own painting, *Beat Depression*, with its movement from darkness into light. A four-year starter and team captain on Ohio State's tennis team, Jeffrey Sparr was diagnosed with OCD (Obsessive-Compulsive Disorder) in college. Since then, painting has become his means of coping with anxiety and mental illness, his bespackled smock a beautifully messy record of drips and drabs of the many colors and ways he pursues beauty, peace, freedom, life.

---

[*] All words in italics from Cliff Richey's *Acing Depression*.

For Cliff and Nancy Richey, arguably the greatest brother-sister duo in the history of tennis, *winning was the be-all and the end-all. It was our life, our business, our religion.* While such a laser-like focus on winning might help one beat depression, it might also, at least for many athletes, lead to some form of depression later in life. How many might be partially cured when they share their story, as Cliff Richey has courageously done, as a kind of guidebook to help others cure themselves? How many more are cured when life becomes not so much winning and losing but helping and supporting others? Some might say that's when anyone's saved from the belly of the whale.

Jorge Mir Mayor, *La Tenista 3040.*

LA TENISTA 3040,

ART BY JORGE MIR MAYOR

La Tenista 3040 is prepared to play in two realms at once: 1) the year 3040, and 2) the mythological past.

The Year 3040: A warming planet, biological weapons, alternate realities, cyborg cities... La Tenista 3040 is prepared. Like those insects crawling over the melting of time in Salvadore Dali's *Persistence of Memory*, La Tenista 3040's eight biomorphic buttons and four biomorph tassels—two for each shoe—will survive any future that may not contain the human race. Hardly any flesh on 3040's arms and legs. Easy to add an AI chip, a bit of superior machinery. Bodies reconstructed, enhanced. His shoes suggest flight in the form of rocket ships, so he can scoot with the best of them, get to any ball, escape any situation on court or off. His emotionless poker face (vaguely reminiscent of those Byzantine saints that transcend time) gives nothing away while his giant *orejas* (ears) take in scraps of information: how other tenistas are preparing, what new technologies are afoot...

The Mythological Realm: Since the creator of La Tenista 3040 is Spanish, he imbued his creation with the secrets of the Spanish style: Miro, Picasso, Dali, Velazquez, Suffering, Sweat, Topspin... In the Spanish style of tennis, you train to hit so many balls in the blazing sun (even hotter in 3040) that you might enter into a mythic realm beyond the body while training the body/mind for whatever it might face. Like the almost-mythological Rafa 2020, La Tenista 3040's Spider-Man strings help him hit so much topspin he can win any match on clay. La Tenista 3040's strings come from both male and female, from Spider-Man and Grandmother Spider. Grandmother Spider (Cherokee) who stole a piece of the sun, stored it in clay, shared it with a world of darkness. La Tenista 3040 remembers it all. He gives thanks for the clay we walk on, the sun that warms it. He gives thanks for hitting balls with a partner. Tennis, he knows, must never become a mindless game played by cyborgs.

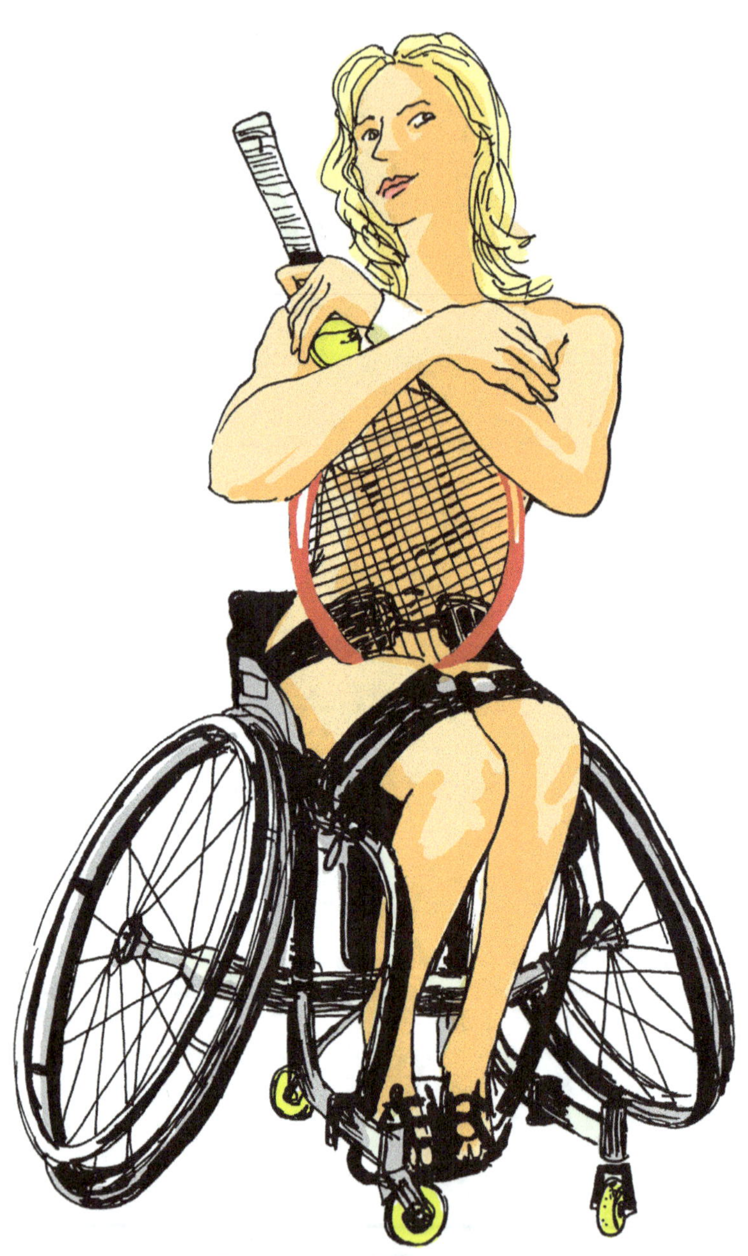

Marielle Durand, *Esther Vergeer*.

ESTHER VERGEER'S BODY,
ART BY MARIELLE DURAND

I cry when I see that picture of me as a little girl. Helpless and alone after the surgery, she must lie on her stomach for a week. No one told Mom or Dad she might need a wheelchair. Alone in the bathroom after another gold medal, I must produce for the mandatory doping test. I need a catheter to pee for the rest of my life. That's worse than losing your legs.[*]

How to feel, how to think, about Esther Vergeer, the greatest female wheelchair player of all time, posing nude for the cover of the ESPN *Body Issue* in 2010. I love how Marielle Durand makes her blonde hair a little blonder, her eyes a little brighter, more open. Is Vergeer engaging us and our thoughts? Is she looking off into the future when posing nude in a wheelchair will no longer be a big deal? I want to read Durand's portrait from where I sit now, fourteen years after the fact. Or better, perhaps, a century after the fact. Women accepted. Disabled people accepted. The body accepted. Bodies are bodies. Nothing more, nothing less. Bodies are bodies unless you're an athlete like Esther Vergeer.

Injury worries performance pressures opponents improving faster faster... Gold medal time. Best thing is to hit high spinners to her. Make it hard to slice. Doesn't look impressive to all those watching, but it's what I should do to win. Why worry about how it all looks? Battle of my life. Year after year without losing. An increasing pressure of being expected to win. New sponsors, too, who only know me as a legend who never loses. I double-fault, miss shots. Family in the stands. Dutch television, too. Why do I feel shame?

---

[*] All the sections in italics are from the language and thoughts of Esther Vergeer from her biography: *Fierce and Vulnerable*.

Easier to pose nude than perform as an athlete? When Donatello sculpts David as the first male nude for over a thousand years, everyone had different ideas about what the nude body might mean: the body as beautiful, the body as pride, the body as sensuality, the body as shame, the body as consciousness, the body as the seat of sin. But what about the body as a vehicle for performance? David beats Goliath, after all. He stands with one foot on his head.

I played with dolls, fought with my brother. My father taught me to ride a bike. Taught me taught me taught me even after we both knew I would never be able to ride a bike.

Jace McTier, *Big John.*

JOHN ISNER'S SERVE,
ART BY JACE MCTIER

The explosion of Isner's serve has happened. Yellow pink green orange burst from the sky. We want to move a little closer or stand back in awe. McTier's vibrant colors mix with our memories of Isner's serve, his thrust up from his legs through his core back and shoulders toward the ridiculous height of ten and a half feet, a movement echoed and enhanced by the surge of brushstrokes behind Isner's right arm.

A thousand aces, a thousand aces, a thousand aces, a thousand aces. That's how the years pass by.

When I need a good laugh, I watch the best players on the planet attempt to return John Isner's serve. You have two options. Neither one good. You must make like a goalkeeper in soccer on penalty kicks and guess where the serve's going or simply react and try to get a racquet on it as serves rocket toward you at different speeds—137 mph, 142, 126, 115, 157.2 (the official fastest serve on record)—the slower slice serves breaking further and further away from you the further back you stand. Some grow desperate, try the slip-on-the-banana-peel option: step way in and take the ball early. The result is the pros often look like beginners. The ball hits the frame. They shank one. This one doesn't get to the net. One ball hits them. Swing and miss. Block a few back. Watch a few more go by.

Yellow hinting gold surrounds John's face like a secular halo, a hint of the divine. From way up on high something comes our way.

Brian Cowlishaw, *"Yes, Tennis Everyone!"*

"YES, TENNIS EVERYONE!"
ART BY BRIAN COWLISHAW

Brian tells me that the inspiration for this artwork comes from Donald Barthelme's story, "The Palace." In this story, the author is in line at a bank in New York City when he notices the yellow check for $84.06 that a Puerto Rican woman holds. Then he notices that there are many other black and brown and white women holding similar checks and he thinks about how little that is for a week's work and what eighty-four dollars might buy. Finally he lights on the crazy idea that this check might buy a good tennis racquet and that everyone might buy a tennis racquet and beat him to death and start a revolution.

Brian cites especially the work's final paragraph: *And I suddenly shouted right out loud, right in front of everyone, in line at Chase Manhattan Fourteenth Street, "Tennis everyone?" And everyone shouted back, "Yes, yes, tennis." And we all set out, the white and black and Puerto Rican women with their tennis racquets, and the clerks and tellers, too, with their racquets, and even the bank officers, in their dark suits, with their racquets, in a long straggle, or friendly mob, in the direction of the palace.*

THREE RIFFS ON BRIAN'S PAINTING

A paycheck for 225 dollars—that's forty hours multiplied by the minimum wage of $7.25 minus fifty dollars the government takes for everyone's needs. A paycheck for 225 dollars for a week's worth of plumping white pillows and replacing white sheets on white beds until all your dreams turn white.

Not much money for carrying white towels through endless white halls of rooms stacked on rooms of elevator floors. You can buy a good racquet for 225 dollars to wield like a lance in the windmill faces of others. They may never see you, never comprehend.

A paycheck for 225 dollars a week—not much for forty hours at the grocery store watching every fourth or fifth customer buy rice and beans and milk with food stamps. You watch each customer pass. You watch other cashiers have their hours cut back to thirty-two hours a week so that no one will pay for their healthcare. You are next in line. You are next in line. You are next in line. You are next in line. You are next in line until everyone around you is next in line. You can buy five or six cheap tennis racquets at Walmart for 225 dollars, pass them out to anyone. Tennis, anyone?

A paycheck as high as 390 dollars—not much for thirty-two or forty or forty-seven or fifty-three hours driving a taxi or bus or midnight Uber, ferrying those who might carry racquets through concrete rivers of smut and smog. You would rather be the saxophone on the radio, the saxophone held close and fingered and blown through gently by an invisible god whose many leaves flutter and fall. September again. The US Open in NYC. All the world's best come here to play tennis. You can buy two very good racquets for 390 dollars, watch them fall in love. More racquets are inevitable. So many racquets you might pass them out to everyone you see while the US Open is played. Open tennis began in NYC in 1968. Arthur Ashe won the tournament, started a revolution so quiet no one knew it was happening. Tennis, everyone?

Andrew Macara, *Tennis Cuba.*

Andrew Macara, *Clay Court Tennis in Lapad, Croatia.*

TENNIS IN CUBA AND CROATIA,
ART BY ANDREW MACARA

Tennis Cuba

A bright yellow house. The sun, the heat, of Cuba. White clothes, brown skin, black hair. Two anonymous boys hit a tennis ball. Tennis in Cuba a victim of the Castro revolution. Hardly anyone played it for years.

Clay Court Tennis in Lapad, Croatia

I would rather watch this painted scene in Lapad, Croatia, than the terrifying serves of Marin Čilić and Goran Ivanišević, Croatia's two Grand Slam champions. Most days now I prefer a simple house with windows, children at play on Earth's red clay, waves and waves of a skilled painter's brushwork in mountains, in trees. Lapad, Croatia, a suburb of Dubrovnik, its sea waters as pure a see-through veil or jewel as any waters I've known.

One of the joys of Macara's paintings is they invite your imagination to travel the world. How is tennis played in every corner of the globe?

Normandie Syken. *Junior Tennis.*

THE WESTSIDE TENNIS CLUB,
ART BY NORMANDIE SYKEN

Pen and ink drawing, watercolor. The real world, the artist's imagination. Life's drift or dialogue between the two. A childhood world of innocence. Moments of hard-to-pin-down adult introspection. Tennis balls dot the courts like an impressionist's flowers. Soft washes of watercolor everywhere. Overly large figures of adult authority—the tennis pros—are made kinder, gentler by both the task they undertake and the surrounding pastoral grass.

Painted entirely in watercolor, the Westside's iconic Tudor house looms quietly in the background, a silent witness to sixty years of US National Championships—later the US Open—from 1915 to 1977. Half-enchanted by Syken's painting, I imagine this historic clubhouse as some godlike, omniscient depository of memory; its two all-seeing eyes suggested by Syken's paint watch player after player from the past: Arthur Ashe who wrote *A Hard Road to Glory*, his three-volume history of the black athlete; Althea Gibson who boxed with her father on the rooftops of Harlem; Bobby Riggs and Don Budge, the two best players in the world, who played in the service during WWII a few miles away from where the Enola Gay took off for Hiroshima...

The Westside Tennis Club. Syken's art. Reality or imagination?

Mark Winter (Chicane), *Kim Clijsters,* **Autographed Sketch.**

KIM CLIJSTERS' SLICED FOREHAND,

ART BY MARK WINTER (CHICANE)

Instructions for hitting Kim's Signature Shot:

Do all of this in one fluid motion

1. Sprint all-out wide to the forehand side for a ball you cannot quite reach.

2. Plant your right leg on the inner side of your shoe, then subtly allow the leg to give way so it can slide up to a foot on concrete.

3. Extend your racquet arm out wide, as far as possible.

4. With your racquet arm held firm, chop or slice downward through the ball as if cutting a carrot or beet. Slice hard enough to produce underspin between 1000 and 2500 rpm. Add sidespin too if you are so inclined.

5. Splay both legs out into the classic splits. (It helps if your mother's a champion gymnast like Kim's.)

6. As a stabilizing balance for your splayed-out legs, set your non-racquet arm down between them as it metamorphoses into the third leg of a temporary tripod, touching down as lightly as a spacecraft might land on the moon.

7. It also helps if you are good-natured, carefree. (Take some time off, have a child, like Kim Clijsters

did before she came back to win her third US Open. Let your smile be a mirror for her smile. Help her develop her own unique signature.)

8. If you hear *ooohs* and *aaahs* from the crowd, ignore them. The key as always in tennis is to recover quickly, prepare for the next shot.

XII: BACKHANDS

Lucy McTier, *Chris Evert's Backhand, A Study in Blue.*

CHRIS EVERT'S BACKHAND, A STUDY IN BLUE,

ART BY LUCY MCTIER

"Light blue is like a flute, dark blue like a cello, and when still darker, it becomes a wonderful double bass."
    – Wassily Kandinsky

Kandinsky saw color in musical/spiritual terms: *Color is a means of exercising direct influence upon the soul. Color is the keyboard. The eye is the hammer, while the soul is a piano of many strings.* Blues lightened by a nuanced dance of whites and yellows make a new unheard music from the flow and swish of Chrissie's dress. How many heads turn while she hits the shot that revolutionized the sport, her two-handed backhand? Did you and your children hit it, too? The color blue's sounds as soft, as subtle, as Kandinsky's or Pan's flute. They lure us forward we know not how. Blues grow darker, deeper, as we approach the edges of the canvas. Evert's body/mind so focused on hitting that classic backhand, she might be playing Bach's suites of stylized dances for solo cello—a light and lively gigue, a moderate and stately allemande, a sensual and slow sarabande.

Cat Lee (Colacat), *Simona Halep's Backhand.*

SIMONA HALEP: THREE EASY-BUT-DIFFICULT-SAFE-BUT-RISKY-CALCULATED-BUT-MINDLESS BACKHANDS,

ART BY CAT LEE (COLACAT)

Situation: Having lost the first set, Simona is serving at 4-4 (15-15) in the second set against Sloane Stephens in the 2018 French Open final.

Sloane floats a weak return just past the service line, so Simona steps in and smacks an eighty-eight-mph sharply angled backhand crosscourt within a foot of the sideline. *I submit that tennis is the most beautiful sport there is and also the most demanding. It requires body control, hand-eye coordination, quickness, flat-out speed, endurance, and that weird mix of caution and abandon we call courage. It also requires smarts. Just one single shot in one exchange in one point of a high-level match is a nightmare of mechanical variables.*[*] Sloane's next ball lands two feet deeper, so Simona steps in aggressively and smacks another backhand crosscourt—subtly recalibrated—seven-to-eight mph slower and two feet further away from the sideline. *No silicon-based RAM yet existent could compute the expansion of variables for even a single exchange; smoke would come out of the mainframe.* Sloane's third shot to Simona's backhand bounces up higher than anticipated while Simona consciously/unconsciously decides or is deciding while adjusting to Sloane's heavier topspin whether to smack a third consecutive backhand crosscourt or go for the riskier backhand down

---

[*] All the words in italics come from my single favorite paragraph on tennis. It is taken from David Foster Wallace's book *String Theory* (pp. 65-66).

the line. *The sort of thinking involved is the sort that can be done only by a living and highly conscious entity, and then it can really be done only unconsciously, i.e., by fusing talent with repetition to such an extent that the variables are combined and controlled without conscious thought.* Nothing worse than losing a fourth consecutive major championship final. Romania's holding its breath. Simona half-strikes half-feathers a Renoir or Monet backhand down the line, a perfect parabolic arc with a sliver of inside-out slice. Sloane anticipated crosscourt. Her left foot slips, almost undetectable, in Halep's favorite city of Paris where no one can explain a Renoir or Monet brushstroke. *In other words, serious tennis is a kind of art.*

Daniel Medvedev's Backhand, Photography by Ray Giubilo.

DANIIL MEDVEDEV'S BACKHAND, A GEMLIKE FLAME,

PHOTOGRAPHY BY RAY GIUBILO

243

Sport as religion, community ritual. Turin, Italy, 2023. Medvedev so fast he's a blur, a blue-green flame in the dark.

We are not honed machines like Medvedev is, his ungodly speed at 6'6" under complete control. His nickname's *the Octopus*. He covers the court like he has eight arms, eight legs. His blue-green sleek shirt leaves traces of where it's been, one moment vanishing into the next. Ray Giubilo creates in his photograph a heightened realism we can never quite see with our limited human vision. These passing visual sensations delight and astonish while blending with our appreciation of Medvedev's skill: blood pulsing, head and mind still, focus on the ball. Athlete and artist and spectator as one. The racquet moves even faster, an extension of the body, technology's wand of wands. Look, look, he's about to slash another hard, flat backhand a foot from each line. *To burn always with this hard, gemlike flame.**

---

* The famous phrase from Walter Pater's *The Renaissance*.

Scott Kish, *Bianca Andreescu's Backhand.*

BIANCA ANDREESCU'S BACKHAND,

ART BY SCOTT KISH

245

Dynamism of a crosscourt backhand. Power, pace, direction. Bianca's arms muscles legs Kish's brushstrokes flying right and left black purple white lines and arcs and physics of movement. No photo no video lives so fully inside where the body was and where it's going. Each wildly controlled black line an echo an expression of Bianca's core Bianca's torso like Apollo's torso in Rilke's eyes as it *bursts from inside like a thousand stars*, launches its yellow missile at ninety mph six inches from the line in the 2019 US Open final, Serena watching its comet tail blaze, the stars the fates knitting and unknitting Bianca's seemingly infinite progression of injuries—knee shoulder arm foot ankle—until maybe, surely, sadly, Bianca is a comet or shooting star.

Brooke Hunter, *Justine Henin's Backhand.*

JUSTINE HENIN'S BACKHAND: MUSIC OF THE SPHERES,
ART BY BROOKE HUNTER

247

I watch Justine in slow motion, the transfer of weight from back to front foot, the coiling uncoiling of the legs the hips the shoulders the core. (Is it true she did a thousand sit-ups a day?) Justine's one-handed backhand, *the most beautiful shot in tennis* (John McEnroe). If all life could be as anticipated yet unexpected. If all life could be so powerful yet loose, free-flowing. If we could somehow record all the spectators' sighs in the world's stadiums the moment after. If we could record all these sighs, apply the zen of John Cage, the minimalism of Steve Reich, the ensuing music would be as sacred as Palestrina's *a cappella* masses, as mysterious as the sound of whales.

Leonardo Luque, *Ken Rosewall's Backhand.*

THE DAO OF
KEN ROSEWALL'S BACKHAND,
ART BY LEONARDO LUQUE

249

The older ones who knew would stop and watch. The younger ones have almost forgotten. Rosewall's slice backhand as repeatable, as simple, as breath itself. If you could hit it at twenty-two, you could hit it at seventy, at eighty. Easy on the body, the mind. Not slice, as most say, but struck almost flat with backspin as subtle as the Dao itself: soft yet hard, power yet touch, yin and yang. Rosewall's backhand can go anywhere; it can do anything or nothing at all: down the line, crosscourt, dink, lob, approach shot, passing shot, rally shot, forcing shot... Oldest major singles champion at thirty-seven, ranked #2 in the world at forty years old. Longest gap between first major and last major in three different Grand Slam championships: Australian, French, US Open. 5'7", 145 pounds. Muscles, breath, elegance. Not color and flash, but simplicity, artistry, line. Poussin, Botticelli, the aging Matisse. As tennis players get older, as their bodies become ghosts of their former splendor, they all dream of Rosewall's backhand.

ARTIST BIOS

Shawn Adair has an MFA in sculpture and is the recipient of an Arkansas Arts Council Individual Fellowship and an award in sculpture from the International Sculpture Center. Shawn enjoys making short films and has an accomplished background in the field of video production. He also creates two-dimensional, three-dimensional, and motion video art that addresses the needs and sensibilities of those with disabilities. You can see some of his many projects on his website at shawnadair.com.

Samuel Brannan: A digital and traditional artist from St. Petersburg, Russia, Sam is a huge tennis fan whose beautiful digital artwork of tennis players is very popular on Instagram. You can see his digital tennis art at redbubble.com/people/SamBrannan/shop.

Louis Briel (US, 1945-2021) studied art at the American Academy in Rome. He specialized in portraits, especially of celebrities. Three of his works hang in the National Portrait Gallery, including his portrait of Arthur Ashe. His portrait of John F. Kennedy was given to Robert F. Kennedy after John Kennedy was assassinated. His portrait of Diana, Princess of Wales, was given to Elton John after Diana's death. Louis Briel also earned a master's degree in Classical Philology at Harvard where he taught Classics as a teaching fellow. He was a writer as well, publishing two novels.

Achille Chiarello was born in Arzignano (Vicenza), Italy, on October 26, 1965. He started artistic activity as a goldsmith after attending the art school in Vicenza. After thirteen years of creating designs of jewelry for other companies, he left the goldsmith's business and began to paint on canvas. Later he resumed some of his goldsmith's techniques, experimenting with wood and new synthetic materials: resins and plastics. Today he paints with different techniques and sculpts on polyurethane, fiberglass, resin, bronze, and alternative materials. You can visit his website at saatchiart.com/achillec_ to see more of his artwork.

Brian Cowlishaw: A professor of English at Northeastern State University in Tahlequah, Oklahoma, Brian Cowlishaw grew up in rural Idaho before earning his Ph.D. at the University of Oklahoma. Inspired by the 2019 NYC exhibit of J. R. R. Tolkien's watercolor art, he took up painting himself. "Why didn't I think of this earlier?" he wonders.

Marielle Durand (Paris, France): Artist, teacher, and active member of Urban Sketchers, Marielle follows a red string: drawing. She watches, analyzes, and shows in her sketchbooks life and people she has met for more than twenty-five years. In Sarajevo, on the top of the Rockefeller Center, down in the Algerian Desert, or in her special "Blue from Auvergne," she tries to capture beauty and moments. Since 2022, she has been invited by the French Parliament to draw the debates and received an Urban Sketchers grant for this project. She takes part in many projects with people in need. Her work can be seen in Europe and the United States. To learn more about Marielle Durand and see more of her art, you can visit her website at Marielle-durand.fr/.

Debra Di Blasi: Known for her innovative prose, Debra Di Blasi has received numerous awards and is the author of eleven books. Notable awards include the 2019 C&R Press Nonfiction Award for her lyric memoir *Selling the Farm: Descants from a Recollected Past* (Sept. 2020), selected for Best Nonfiction Books 2020-2021 by *Entropy Magazine*; Thorpe Menn Literary Excellence Award for *Drought & Say What You Like* (New Directions); the &NOW Award for "*The Jiri Chronicles* excerpts" (FC2/Univ. Alabama Press); *Diagram* Innovative Writing Award; and a Christopher Isherwood Fiction Fellowship. In the world of the visual arts, Debra Di Blasi took a BFA in painting and later worked as art critic and contributing writer for *The Pitch*, *SOMA Magazine*, and *The New Art Examiner*. Her visual and multimedia art has been exhibited at museums and galleries in the US and online. *Nostos Journal of Poetry, Fiction and Art* published a portfolio of her Chinese brush painting in Volume III 2019, including cover art. You can learn more about Debra Di Blasi and her wide-ranging work at debradiblasi.com.

Ted Dimond is both a tennis professional and the leading painter of contemporary tennis stars on the WTA and ATP tours. He has been tennis director at the John McEnroe Tennis Academy, and his artwork hangs on the walls of numerous Grand Slam champions. At ATP tour trophy ceremonies, his tennis portraits are often presented to the tournament champion. At the US Open, Dimond hosts his annual "Art at the Open" show where you can meet the artist and see some of the top players in the game. Ted has also painted for sporting events like the Super Bowl, the Masters, and the Kentucky Derby. He will be showing his work in Paris for the Olympics this year (2024). You can learn more about Ted's art and life on his website at teddimond.com and you can follow him on Instagram at teddimond_art.

Harold Edgerton (1903-1990) was an American scientist and researcher, a professor of electrical engineering at MIT, and an influential photographer who helped change the course of photography. He patented the stroboscope—a high-powered repeatable flash device—in 1949, the device used in his photograph of Pancho Gonzales. His books include *Flash! Seeing the Unseen by Ultra High-Speed Photography* (1939), *Electronic Flash, Strobe* (1969), *Moments of Vision: The Stroboscopic Revolution in Photography* (1979), and *Sonar Images* (1986). His revolutionary photographs were included in the first exhibition of photography at the Museum of Modern Art in 1937. Also known as "Papa Flash," Edgerton was awarded the U.S. National Medal of Science in 1973 and received the International Center of Photography Infinity Award for Lifetime Achievement in 1987.

James Fawcette is a tennis fan, photographer, and serial entrepreneur in denial about being retired. You can check out his many photographs of ATP and WTA tennis players at jfawcette.myportfolio.com/work.

Ray Giubilo started his career as a tennis photographer at the 1989 Australian Open and since then has covered more than 120 Grand Slam tournaments and more than 150 other tennis events including Davis and Fed Cup ties and ATP/WTA tournaments. In 2011 he published his fourth book, *IL RE DELLA TERRA*, a book dedicated to the career of Rafa Nadal, and in 2017 a new, updated version of *ROGER FEDERER, il N.1 di sempre*. His work has been published in many editorial publications around the world and he is the staff photographer for *IL TENNIS ITALIANO*, the world's oldest tennis magazine. You can visit tennisphotographer.com to view his image bank of tennis photographs.

Miki de Goodaboom: Born in the French Pyrenees, Miki de Goodaboom moved to Göttingen, Germany, at nineteen to study mathematics and physics. After graduating, she worked for many years in German industry as a mathematician and consultant until she moved to Andalucia, Spain, where she lives now. A self-taught artist, Miki kept creating more and more art until it finally became her full-time profession. She most enjoys painting sport themes since she loves movement and the challenge of reducing it to two dimensions on paper or canvas. You can check out her art from the world of sports on her website at miki-fonvielle.pixels.com/collections/sport+art.

Stephen Gulbis is an artist/illustrator living in the UK. Known widely as "the Football Artist," Steve studied Graphic Design at Bath Academy of Art. His clients include Manchester United, Liverpool, Tottenham Hotspur, Football Association, USA Soccer Federation, English Football League, Scottish Professional Football League, New Balance, Diadora, and many more. His portrait of Jana Novotná and the Duchess of Kent is part of "The Ace Heroes Series" commissioned by the Lawn Tennis Association. You can learn more about Steve and his work on his website at thefootballartist.com.

Enrique Miguez Huguenin was a Mexican and Swiss national (father Mexican and mother Swiss) born and raised in Mexico. He was a pioneer of the technique of using cement in the sculptural form, including the use of two colors—yellow ochre and red—with a very high polish after it was completed. Through the combination of colorants and stone mixtures, some very warm and pleasing color tones can be achieved. The most popular method of coloring cement sculpture is that of mixing the colorant with the wet cement. His statue of Rafael Osuna was first unveiled by the president of Mexico, José López Portillo.

Tom Humberstone is an award-winning comic artist and illustrator based in Edinburgh. His debut graphic novel, *Suzanne: The Jazz Age Goddess of Tennis*, was published by Avery Hill in September 2022. He writes and draws non-fiction comics for the Ignatz award-winning *The Nib*, as well as the *New Statesman*, *Vox*, *Buzzfeed*, and others. He is the editor and publisher of the critically acclaimed UK comics anthology *Solipsistic Pop* and co-editor of *Over The Line: An Introduction to Poetry Comics*. You can learn more about Tom Humberstone and his work on his website at tomhumberstone.com.

Brooke Hunter is an American Cypriot who grew up in the Midwest. She moved to California in 2016 after receiving a scholarship to study at Laguna College of Art and Design. She received her BFA in Drawing and Painting spring of 2020 and is currently teaching in Santa Ana at the Orange County School of the Arts (OCSA) and from her private studio in Fullerton, CA. Brooke enjoys painting subjects such as the human figure and still life. Her goal is to capture those feelings and thoughts that are so often just fleeting moments and turn them into something that feels grounded, cohesive, and relatable. You can learn more about Brooke and her art at brookehunterart.com.

Carol Jacobsen has been painting since childhood. She has studied art at the University of Minnesota, where she earned a B.A., as well as at the Minneapolis College of Art and Design, the College of Marin, and San Francisco State. Color is her main passion. As she writes of her art: "Whether I'm doing abstract or more realistic paintings, I always use color to express the feelings I want to convey. As I work on an idea, I start by layering the various colors, then get into a meditative state, which gives expression to the images and stories of the painting." Her art has been awarded Best of Show by the International Society of Acrylic Painters in 2005 and has been featured in *Artweek*. Many of her artworks are held in corporate spaces and private collections both in the United States and internationally. The portrait of Althea Gibson in this book is from her "Women of Color and Accomplishment" series. You can learn more about Carol and her work at caroljacobsen.org.

Victor Jerez worked for years in the Port of Algeciras as a stevedore, but it was not those hours of sunshine that called him to his vocation. Rather, it was the light bulbs in his garage, late at night, where he practiced his passion: painting movie posters. Shortly after, he decided to paint live. At the beginning it was in small parties and local events (in Algeciras, Sotogrande). Then bigger events came and, without realizing it, he saw himself painting George Clooney, Keith Richards, and Carlos Jean. Sporting event painting came later. Now he's often called "The Painter of Athletes," capturing on canvas live athletes such as Rafa Nadal, Sergio Garcia, and Novak Djokovic. You can learn more about Victor Jerez and his art at victorjerez.com.

Scott Kish: Currently residing in Toronto, Scott obtained his Bachelor of Science degree in Kinesiology from the University of Waterloo, where he specialized in human anatomy and visual information processing. Applying his knowledge of applied anatomy and biomechanics, Scott takes a contemporary approach to his art, capturing the synergy of movement, energy, and emotion of the subject matter. Scott's work enhances many public spaces, residing in a number of collections, both corporate and private.

Jota Leal (Venezuela): Jota's unique style comes about from his remarkable painting skill and a probing sense of the subject's soul. As *Juxtapoz Magazine* put it: "Jota Leal probes the subconscious, showing that depth can be shown with humor and whimsy." Jota's first art book, *About Face, The Art of Jota*, was released in 2015. He currently exhibits at the Gallery of Music & Art in the Forum Shops at Caesar's Palace, Las Vegas, and at Sally Fine Art in Taipei, Taiwan.

Cat Lee (aka Colacat): A self-taught artist, Cat Lee (Colacat) produces a wide variety of popular art on tennis. You can check out her tennis art and products at her Best Tennis Fanart Center at colacatlee.com.

Joan LeMay (born 1979 in Houston, Texas) is a portraitist and illustrator who is interested in pattern, gesture, Byzantine halos, and capturing the true soul of the subject she's painting. She loves painting people, animals, plants, and things (a kind of anthropomorphic approach to portraiture) in equal measure, and packs referential objects, color-based symbolism, and other subject-specific elements into the often-busy backgrounds of her work in order to reflect the life of the person or creature depicted. She is currently focusing on work that celebrates who and what soothes us and brings us joy—portraiture of dear friends, over-the-top portraits of beloved TV and pop culture personalities and public role models, food, fellow artists, and portraits of medications. Much in demand as a portrait artist, Joan LeMay's work has been exhibited internationally for over a decade. To learn more about her extensive list of clients, the many publications where her art has appeared, and, most importantly, to see more of her work—and thus feel a little better about being alive—you can visit her website at joanlemay.com.

Tom Lohner: The wildly inventive and popular Austrian artist, Tom Lohner, has the following credo: "Where passion pulls—follow. Never question this—it may be the only chance in your life to be truly alive." Celebrated for paintings that combine a traditional medium of acrylic colors and futurist aesthetics, Tom Lohner is perhaps most famous for his "Art of Hard Rock" series, where he transformed thirteen iconic rock stars into animals, a show that toured throughout Europe in various Hard Rock Cafes. His clients include David Alaba, Dan Aykroyd, Arnold Schwarzenegger, Hard

Rock Cafe, BMW, and many more. His current work includes participation at the world's fair in Japan/Osaka next year (2025), as he is commissioned by the Austrian government to create an artwork that combines both cultures. The artwork will stay in Japanese possession and will be exhibited long-term in Osaka. To learn more about Tom Lohner and his work, you can visit his website at tomlohner.com.

Leonardo Luque, a retired Colombian naval officer, earned his fine arts degree in 2012 from Jorge Tadeo Lozano University in Bogota, Colombia. A highly ranked Colombian player in the ITF world rankings for senior men, Leo has drawn all his life and is especially interested in the beauty and motion of the human body. After traveling through China and Panama, he settled down with his family in 2014 in Boca Raton, Florida.

Andrew Macara studied contemporary modern British Art for a short period with Leonard Fuller at the St. Ives School of Painting amongst the Cornwall Art Galleries but considers himself to be predominantly a self-taught artist. He travels extensively gathering images for paintings from around the world, but his native Derbyshire continues to feature in many paintings—particularly the winter scenes. Other subjects with strong demand are Andrew's British seaside paintings. Ken Howard describes Macara's paintings exceptionally well: "I have known and admired the work of Andrew Macara for many years, both from his many one-man exhibitions and also his work so often seen in the Royal Academy Summer Exhibition. Although he has painted many different subjects over the years, the subject is always incidental to light. His pictures glow and as with all the best paintings of light they never describe; they are always an equivalent for light—the light comes from the canvas. As well as being full of light they are full of life. Whether it be life on the beach, in the playground, or in the zoo, he simplifies but always captures the essence of his subject; his work is full of movement, atmosphere, and space. Andrew's work is deservedly popular for he touches the everyday joy of life." You can see more of Andrew Macara's work on his website at macara.com.

Jorge Mir Mayor: Director of Tennis at the Escuelas Tenis Real Club, Jorge Mir Mayor is one of the leading teachers and commentators on tennis in Spain. Over the course of thirty years as a director of tennis in Spain, Jorge Mir Mayor has received multiple honors and awards, including the awards for Best Tennis Professional, Best Tennis Director, and Best Tennis Club in Spain. He also paints in his free time.

Jace McTier: The son of renowned portrait artist Lucy McTier, Jace McTier's first sporting painting was commissioned following the 1996 Equestrian Olympic trials in Thomson, Georgia. His first lithograph of a hunt scene, complete with twenty hounds and four horses and riders, benefited Easter Seals. Soon he was commissioned to paint a large landscape for the John Deere Corporation with 5,000 limited-edition prints—and was well on his way as an established artist. Beginning at the age of sixteen, Jace was "knocking out" large oil commissions.

Recently hailed as the next Leroy Neiman, McTier's bold color and powerful use of impasto ranks him among today's leading sporting artists. With work collected by such clients as Angelo Dundee and George Foreman to corporate commissions, his paintings benefit charities through the sale of his original work as well as print sales. A recent project includes a joint venture with the Press On Fund and Jack Nicklaus to aid in finding a cure for childhood cancer. Jace McTier's art has been exhibited multiple times publicly along with Leroy Neiman's original paintings. To learn more about Jace and see more of his art, you can visit his website at mctierart. com.

Lucy McTier: A portraitist since 1979, one of the many highlights of Lucy McTier's career in art was her opportunity to paint President Ronald Reagan and present him with his portrait in the Oval Office of the White House along with her then-five-year-old son, Jace, and her husband, David, in 1985. Lucy has work hanging in over 350 public and private collections, and in several gallery locations. Her work is primarily in oil on linen, but she offers prints of her work as well. You can learn more about her and see more of her at mctierart.com.

Ken Meyer Jr. is a freelance commercial and comic artist whose work has appeared in *Spectrum*. He has done work for a wide range of clients, including Sony Online, the American Cancer Society, the Savannah College of Art and Design, Marvel Comics, and Bell Helmets. You can see more of his work on his website at kenmeyerjr.com.

National Portrait Gallery: Two works of art from the Smithsonian's National Portrait Gallery are featured in this book: the painting of Arthur Ashe by Louis Briel and the drawing of Donald Budge by Samuel Woolf. Erin Beasley, the NPG's Digital Image Rights & Reproduction Specialist, was especially helpful in providing me with contact information and help in procuring these paintings. The National Portrait Gallery was authorized and founded by Congress in 1962 with the mission to acquire and display portraits of individuals who have made significant contributions to the history, development, and culture of the people of the United States. Today, the Smithsonian's National Portrait Gallery continues to narrate the multifaceted and ever-changing story of America through the individuals who have shaped its culture.

Michael Newberry (born 1956 in the US) is an American romantic figurative painter living in Idyllwild, California, and is the author of *Evolution Through Art* and *Newberry Color Theory*. His art integrates passion, mind, and visual perception. Important influences are Rembrandt, van Gogh, and contemporary sculptor Martine Vaugel. He started painting at eleven years old and sold his first work at seventeen. Thousands of his drawings, charcoals, pastels, acrylics, oil sketches, and definitive works have been collected worldwide. Notable collectors are Chan Luu, Lori and Brian Teacher, and philosopher Stephen Hicks. He says: "Since falling in love with Rembrandt's magic as an adolescent, I have been on a life-long quest to express through art my perceptual, emotional, and mental discoveries." In tennis he was the 1974 California State Champion, member of the USC 1976 NCAA Championship Team, and had wins over top-100 world-ranked players: Ramesh Krishnan, Louk Sanders, and Haroon Ismail. To learn more about his life and art, you can visit newberryarchive.wordpress.com.

Leslie Palafox: The beautiful painting of Rafael Osuna in this book is done by Leslie Palafox, the wife of Osuna's long-time doubles partner, Antonio Palafox. Antonio Palafox and Rafael Osuna won many doubles titles together, including Wimbledon and the US Open. Together they formed the only Mexican Davis Cup team to reach the Davis Cup finals. Antonio Palafox was also the former coach of John McEnroe.

Lady Pink was born in Ecuador, raised in NYC, and currently resides in the countryside north of the city. In 1979 she started writing graffiti and soon became well known as the only female capable of competing with the boys in the graffiti subculture. Pink painted subway trains from 1979 to 1985 and in 1982 had a starring role in the motion picture *Wild Style*. That role and her other significant contributions to graffiti have made her a cult figure in the hip-hop subculture. Her highly prized paintings can be seen in important fine art collections such as those of the Whitney Museum, the MET in New York City, the Brooklyn Museum, the Museum of Fine Art in Boston, and the MoMA.

Giada Ilenia Pinna (aka Ely) is from Sardinia, Italy. She started drawing and painting as a child and hasn't stopped since. She loves drawing fantasy characters, comics, manga, portraying people, painting landscapes, animals, flowers, and above all drawing with digital and acrylic techniques. Ely tries to capture all the beauty of life from small daily gestures. You can see more of Ely's art, especially her unique portraits of women, on her Instagram account @ yleniaely.art.

Katie Wall Podracky holds degrees in art and biology from Washington and Lee University in Lexington, Virginia. She paints bright, lively work full of color, movement, and impressionistic touches. Primarily known for her landscapes, Podracky's work is collected across the United States and featured in the permanent collections of multiple universities and corporations. She releases new collections of original art and fine art prints and teaches painting workshops on her website at katiewallart.com throughout the year.

Keith Richardson achieved a career-high ATP singles ranking of No. 63 while playing on the ATP tour in the 1970s. He has career wins over Kevin Curren (twice), John Lloyd, Eliott Teltscher, and Eddie Dibbs. He has been inducted into the following Halls of Fame: South Carolina, North Carolina, Appalachian State University Athletic Hall of Fame and the York County (S.C.) Sports Hall of Fame.

Al Satterwhite is a veteran photographer who has been published in major magazines such as *Life*, *Look*, *Sports Illustrated*, *Time*, and many others. Published photographic books include *The Cozumel Diary* (adventures with Hunter S. Thompson in Mexico), *Titans* (Muhammad Ali & Arnold Schwarzenegger), *The Racers* (the Golden Age of endurance motor racing), *Carroll Shelby* (one of the most iconic racing giants of the sixties), *Paul Newman: Blue-Eyed Cool*, *The Rolling Stones Icons*, *Lights! Camera! Advertising!*, and *Satterwhite on Color and Design*. He's currently working on two more books.

Satterwhite's stark black-and-white imagery and signature style of color and design are represented in the permanent collections of the Smithsonian National Portrait Gallery, Museum of Fine Arts Houston, Santa Barbara Museum of Art, Los Angeles County Museum of Art (LACMA), George Eastman House, Polaroid Collection, National Museum of African American History and Culture, Ft. Wayne Museum of Art, as well as numerous private collections. Satterwhite's iconic photograph of Hunter Thompson was included in the important Smithsonian show and book, *American Cool*. Satterwhite's passion and curiosity in capturing images has expanded to motion pictures and television advertising. Seldom without a camera in hand, Satterwhite lives in New York City with his wife, Valery, and two Zen-Masters, both of them cats.

Robin Sellick grew up in the historic mining town of Broken Hill in the outback of Australia. After a stint in New York working as an assistant to many of the leading photographers of that period—including Annie Leibovitz, Mark Seliger, and Mary Ellen Mark—he returned to Sydney in 1994 and quickly established himself in the Australian market, shooting for all the major magazine publications including *Vogue* and *Rolling Stone*. His creative use of light came to be seen as a trademark feature of his work and his style became more influential as Australia's magazine market became more sophisticated. He was instrumental in developing a distinctive style of photography for *Who Weekly* as it transformed into a glossy, full-color magazine and was the first photographer to be commissioned to shoot in Australia for Marie Claire.

Robin's portraits have been exhibited internationally including at the National Portrait Gallery in Copenhagen and have appeared on the covers of magazines such as *Q, NME*, and *German Rolling Stone*. Subjects range from Cate Blanchett and Steve Irwin to Kylie Minogue and Radiohead. Commercial clients include HSBC, Rolex, and BHP. The National Portrait Gallery of Australia has seventeen of his portraits in their permanent collection, of which the John Newcombe portrait is one.

Bogdan Shiptenko from Ukraine is a watercolor artist of urban landscapes and figurative painting. In his works he combines acrylic, markers, watercolors, and graphics. The artist's paintings are in the contemporary collections of such countries as the UAE, USA, Canada, France, Germany, Great Britain, Slovenia, etc. He collaborates with the O Wallpapers as an artist and graphic designer, and he has engaged in projects with such companies as Volkswagen, Renault, and Epicenter. Of his art, he writes: "Figurative painting has become the space in which I reflect through my works the perceptions of the environment, activities peoples, and where I view this on a deep societal scale. There are many figures in my paintings, where each character lives separately, but in an ideological sense, they are all united in a common activity that brings them together and carries a meaningful message." You can see more of Bogdan Shiptenko's work on Instagram @bogdan_shiptenko.

Mark Shorter is Head of Sculpture and Spatial Practice at the Victorian College of the Arts, University of Melbourne. His work questions dominant narratives around landscape, gender, and the body in works of sculpture, painting, installation, video, and performance. His numerous paintings of the body parts of famous Aussie tennis players in this collection are the result of two years of intensive collaboration. You can learn more about Mark Shorter's many projects at markshorter.com.au.

Nial Smith: Based in Edinburgh, Scotland, Nial Smith is a designer/artist/illustrator/filmmaker. He is most famous in tennis circles for his witty spoof movie posters of Andy Murray (and other players) such as *Crocodile Dunblane.* You can see his work at nialsmith.co.uk.

Hazel Soan is a British artist well known for her watercolours of people and wildlife. She works out of studios in both London and Cape Town and on location throughout the world. She is known particularly for her direct wet-into-wet watercolour approach and portrayal of movement. The author of twenty-four books, she became popular for her television role as an Art Expert on Channel 4's Watercolour Challenge and her own series, Anglia TV's *Splash of Colour.* Her work is held in many private and public collections worldwide, including the National Portrait Gallery, the Lister Institute, the Chelsea and Westminster Hospital, the British Embassy in Ankara, and the EU Delegation in Windhoek. Her numerous solo exhibitions have taken place in London and the UK, Venezuela, Namibia, and Zimbabwe. You can see her work and learn more about her on her website at allsoanup.com.

Jeffrey Sparr: A mental health advocate and self-taught artist, Jeffrey Sparr was a four-year starter and team captain on the Ohio State University tennis team. When he graduated in 1985, he was the third-winningest player in Ohio State history. Diagnosed with Obsessive-Compulsive Disorder (OCD) in college, Jeff battled with this disease for many years before discovering, on a whim, that painting dramatically subdued the symptoms of his OCD, providing a creative outlet and sense of control. Sparr has been crowned the "Forrest Gump" of painting: Forrest didn't stop running; Sparr hasn't stopped painting. This discovery changed the course of Jeff's life. Ever since then, Jeff has been on a mission to help others through the arts, founding—along with his cousin—the nonprofit organization PeaceLove. You can learn more about Jeff Sparr's art on his website at jeffreysparr.com. You can learn more about Jeff Sparr's work as a mental health advocate at peacelove.org.

Normandie Syken is an illustrator from Queens, New York. She attended the Frank Sinatra School of the Arts and earned her BFA in the illustration program at the School of Visual Arts. Her work has been displayed in galleries and public places such as the SVA Chelsea Gallery and the Forest Hills Gardens Corporation. Recently her artist's books, prints, and illustrations have been acquired by established collections across the US and UK. Normandie likes to draw from life and her imagination using pen and watercolor as well as experimenting with different printmaking techniques. You can see more of her work on her website at normandiesyken.com.

Christina Tarkoff: "With my paintings," Christina Tarkoff writes, "I try to tell stories that cross traditional barriers such as gender, age, income, education, and race to help us understand the most important *art* of all—*the art of being human.*" The portrait of Billie Jean King in this book is part of her "Women Who Shatter Barriers" series. You can learn more about Christina and her award-winning artwork on her website at christinatarkoff.com.

Wimbledon Lawn Tennis Museum: This must-see stop for all tennis fans holds a collection of nearly 1,075,000 items, chronicling the history of lawn tennis and the championships, Wimbledon. It boasts the largest collection of any tennis museum in the world. My thanks to Sarah Frandsen, Photo Library Manager, for allowing me to use the photo of Toupie Lowther from their collection.

Mark Winter is a New Zealand award-winning artist, cartoonist, designer, and filmmaker who lives in London. His cartoons, produced under the pen name "Chicane," appear regularly in a number of publications both in the UK and internationally. He has combined his drawing prowess with a love of tennis and collecting autographs over the past twenty-five years to accumulate an extensive gallery of signed player sketches. You can see more of Mark Winter's work on his website at chicanepictures.com.

Samuel Woolf (US, 1880-1948) is well known for his portraits of influential figures such as Donald Budge, which now reside in the National Portrait Gallery. He is also famous for his many paintings of war done during WWI and WWII.

David Yarrow is recognized as one of the world's bestselling photographers. He has found his true comfort zone in capturing the animal and human world in a fresh and creative way. A key part of his success has been creating art through partnerships with a philanthropic objective and this has enabled him to work with leading figures in sport, fashion, and Hollywood such as Cindy Crawford, Cara Delevingne, Ciara and Russell Wilson, and Alessandra Ambrosio. Since 2019, charitable donations from the sale of David's images have exceeded $15 million.

David Yarrow was born in Glasgow, Scotland, in 1966. He took up photography at an early age and as a twenty-year-old found himself working as a photographer for *The London Times* on the pitch at the World Cup Final in Mexico City. On that day, David took the famous picture of Diego Maradona holding the World Cup and, as a result, was subsequently asked to cover the Olympics and numerous other sporting events. His distinctive work in recent years has earned him an ever-growing following amongst art collectors. Yarrow is now represented by some of the top contemporary galleries around the world. In the autumn of 2022, Rizzoli published David's third book, *Storytelling*. For more on David Yarrow's life and work, you can visit his website at davidyarrow.photography.

AUTHOR BIOS

Scott Barclay: A Scot and a huge Andy Murray fan, Scott Barclay is the co-host of the podcast Murry Musings. You can follow his very popular account on X (Twitter) at BarclayCard18.

Coach Robert Cox: In his twenty-six years as head tennis coach at the University of Arkansas, Coach Cox led Arkansas to nine NCAA Tournament appearances as a team, six regional finals, and one Round of 16 appearance. He had eleven teams ranked among the top thirty-five in the nation and produced thirteen All-Americans.

Joel Drucker: One of the most knowledgeable and talented writers on any sport, Joel Drucker has written superbly and widely on tennis since 1982. As part of Tennis Channel's team since the network started airing in 2003, he has produced an endless stream of work as a writer, story editor, and producer on all things tennis. His writing has also appeared in many other venues, including the *New York Times*, *Tin House*, *Huffington Post*, *Salon*, *Tennis Magazine*, and *Racquet Magazine*. In 2016, he was named historian-at-large by the International Tennis Hall of Fame. Published in 2004, his book *Jimmy Connors Saved My Life* is one of the best books on tennis ever written. To learn more about Joel Drucker and his many accomplishments as a writer and producer, you can visit his website at joeldrucker.com.

David Hall: A member of both the International Tennis Hall of Fame and the Australian Sporting Hall of Fame, David Hall is one of the greatest wheelchair players in the history of the sport. Ranked #1 in the world for six different years, he has won thirty-three major championships. You can learn more about him on his website at hallymustang.com. You can learn more about wheelchair tennis and David's journey in the sport at letsrollwheelchairtennis.com.

Mark Mathabane: A *New York Times* bestselling author, Mark Mathabane appeared as a guest on Oprah Winfrey's show to speak about his influential work, *Kaffir Boy*, and served as a White House Fellow under Bill Clinton (who had also read *Kaffir Boy*). In addition to being the author of numerous books, Mark is a motivational speaker. He recently spoke at the National Press Club in Washington, D.C., on November 6, 2023, in honor of the fiftieth anniversary of Ashe's historic visit to South Africa in 1973. His topic was how Ashe was the first free black man he had ever seen as a thirteen-year-old, and how his visit inspired Mark to make the tough choices that eventually saved his life.

Jimmy Miller strings racquets at Swetka's Tennis Shop in Mountain View, California. In the piece he wrote for this book, "String Therapy," Jimmy states that he has strung over 80,000 racquets while practicing the craft he learned from his father. Jimmy played college tennis at Santa Clara University, where he earned his degree in Psychology. His father, Greg Miller, was the head tennis pro at the Los Gatos Swim and Racquet Club.

ACKNOWLEDGMENTS

I am grateful for the editors of the following journals where many of the pieces included here, with slight modifications, first appeared: *Mulberry Fork Review, Cagibi,* and *Another Chicago Magazine.* I am also grateful for the work of the *National Men's Tennis Association,* where many of these pieces also first appeared.

Over the last seven years, I have collaborated with many artists from around the world on this project. I cannot thank them enough, nor can I possibly name them all here. Two of these artists, though, deserve special mention because of the sheer amount of time I spent with them. I met Leonardo Luque at a tennis tournament in El Paso when I was just beginning work on this project. A highly ranked tennis player from Colombia, Leo was also an artist who provided me with many drawings and paintings of tennis players over a lengthy period of time. Two of his works appear in this book. The Australian artist, Mark Shorter, from the University of Melbourne, sent me a new oil painting of an Australian tennis legend about every three months for over two years. Chapter 10 of this book, entitled "Aussies and Body Parts," is devoted to our collaboration.

Erin Beasley from the Smithsonian's National Portrait Gallery was especially helpful in providing me with contact information for different artists and help in procuring two paintings from their collection. Sarah Frandsen and Malin Lunden from the Wimbledon Lawn Tennis Museum answered all my questions and provided me with a high-resolution photograph of Toupie Lowther to use in this book. I am thankful for these two institutions and their willingness to share their collections. Gus Kayafas, who oversees a collection of Harold Edgerton photographs, provided me with Harold Edgerton's photograph of Pancho Gonzales as well as additional information on this photograph. He also helped edit my short piece on Edgerton's photograph.

Two of my colleagues at Northeastern State University, Dr. Diane Boze (Art History) and Christopher Murphy (Creative Writing), offered both encouragement and a great deal of insightful advice on individual pieces. Three editors from Atmosphere Press played important roles in improving the manuscript I sent them. Nate Hansen helped tighten the contents and prose of this book further with all his cogent advice. Ronaldo Alves was extraordinarily patient in working with me to include as many artists as possible on the book cover. Alex Kale answered my seemingly endless questions about artwork and high-resolution images and how it all might work in the book.

Thanks as well to Emily Nelson, my oldest daughter, who helped me download high-resolution files and save them whenever I could not figure out the technology. Finally, I owe the greatest debt to Anne Linebarger, my youngest daughter, who read through four or five of these pieces almost every month for four or five years, helping me eliminate the less promising pieces and ideas of the many I presented her each month. When I got nearer to the final draft of each work, her suggestions for improving the language and content of each piece were almost always spot-on.

ABOUT ATMOSPHERE PRESS

Founded in 2015, Atmosphere Press was built on the principles of Honesty, Transparency, Professionalism, Kindness, and Making Your Book Awesome. As an ethical and author-friendly hybrid press, we stay true to that founding mission today.

If you're a reader, enter our giveaway for a free book here:

SCAN TO ENTER
BOOK GIVEAWAY

If you're a writer, submit your manuscript for consideration here:

SCAN TO SUBMIT
MANUSCRIPT

And always feel free to visit Atmosphere Press and our authors online at atmospherepress.com. See you there soon!

ABOUT THE AUTHOR

After leaving a career in music (classical guitar) due to injury, **DAVID LINEBARGER** earned a Ph.D. in English at UC Davis before becoming a Professor of Humanities at Northeastern State University in Tahlequah, Oklahoma. His publications include scholarly essays on Wallace Stevens and Modern Music, poems in over thirty journals, and two small collections of poetry: *War Stories* and *Bed of Light*. A nationally ranked tennis player in his age group, his recent nonfiction writings on tennis and art have appeared in *Cagibi* and *Another Chicago Magazine*.

www.ingramcontent.com/pod-product-compliance
Lightning Source LLC
Chambersburg PA
CBHW070851160726
48004CB00003B/1025